INTROD

Introducing Jesus

ROY CLEMENTS

KINGSWAY PUBLICATIONS
EASTBOURNE

First published 1986
This revised edition 1992

Cover design by W. James Hammond

ISBN 0–85476–321–X

Printed in Great Britain for
KINGSWAY PUBLICATIONS LTD
1 St Anne's Road, Eastbourne, E Sussex BN21 3UN by
Clays Ltd, St. Ives plc
Typeset by Watermark, Crostwight, Norfolk

Contents

Foreword

Nothing is more important for men and women in secularised Western society than to introduce them to Jesus. It is not that people have investigated and then rejected Jesus; it is nearly always that they have never really examined his life and his claims.

This is what Dr Roy Clements does in his book. He opens up for us the seven main discources of Jesus, which John records in his gospel. It is no wonder that Cambridge University students flock in their hundreds to Eden Baptist Church to listen to Roy Clements. For here is Christian teaching at its best.

To begin with, Roy Clements is *faithful* to the biblical text. He knows Greek but does not parade his knowledge. He has read the commentaries, but does not follow them slavishly. He is not afraid to adopt unfashionable positions, if integrity requires him to do so. For he interprets the text in both its historical and its biblical contexts. When there are alternative possibilities, he tells us not only which he chooses, but why. I admire his robust common sense and balanced judgement.

Secondly, Roy Clements is *contemporary* in his applications. He moves freely in the world of Marx and Freud, Satre and William Golding, of religious pluralism and scientific secularism, of empty existentialism and revolutionary violence. He is also familiar with the modern theological and christological debates. It is against the background of all this intellectual ferment that he invites us to listen afresh to the message of Jesus, and to grasp its relevance to our lives.

Thirdly, he is *serious* in his purpose. True, he knows the foibles of fallen beings, and sometimes pokes fun at them. But there is nothing flippant here. For Dr Clements is concerned that we should see Jesus. He wants to get behind the discourses to the speaker, behind the popular image to the real person. He portrays him as John witnesses to him, defends him against his detractors, and commends him to modern men and women. No attempt has been made to disguise the fact that these chapters began their life as sermons. So the preacher still addresses us directly and outspokenly. Some readers will surely be brought by the Holy Spirit to faith in Jesus. Others will have their faith clarified and strengthened. None of us can fail to be enriched.

John Stott
December 1985

Preface

This book began its life as a series of sermons preached at Eden Baptist Church, Cambridge in 1984. These were subsequently transcribed and published under the title 'Introducing Jesus' in 1986.

The decision of Kingsway Publications to produce a second edition has provided the opportunity to revise and abridge the text. This had been done in order to make the book more relevant to the non-Christian reader. Material which was chiefly of interest to those who had already found their way to faith has been deleted, as have most references to internal debates within the Christian church. As a result the book is now considerably shorter, but hopefully more accessible to the kind of audience which the apostle John himself most definitely had in mind when he wrote his gospel.

The text, however, remains substantially that of the original sermons. And the debt I expressed in the preface to the first edition to the friends who worked hard to prepare those sermons for publication is no less appropriate to this present volume. Pat Blake typed the manuscripts; Paul Riddington prepared the original tape-recordings and handled a great deal of related administrative work; Christopher Catherwood edited the text for publication. It is their hope, as it is mine, that the end result of our labour will be that others become committed to Jesus.

Roy Clements
Cambridge 1992

1

Born Twice

John 3:1–21

Have you noticed how popular television chat shows are becoming? You know the sort of thing I mean. The set is always the same. There is a big armchair, a sofa, a coffee table with a carafe of water on it. On one side sits the interviewer, on the other some celebrity or other. And then for fifteen minutes or so, they talk. John Freeman pioneered the format with a programme called *Face to Face* back in the 1960s. Since then Michael Parkinson and Terry Wogan have developed the idea. It is surprising in a way that a population fed on the high drama of soap operas and cops-and-robbers can still find mere conversation so entertaining!

It must I think have something to do with the desire people have to get to know famous people more intimately. We have come to realise that publicity, ironically enough, often conceals a person's true identity, even in the process of making them what we call 'well-known'.

Perhaps that is why President Woodrow Wilson once told students in Princeton that he never read a book if it was possible to talk for half an hour to the man who wrote it. Conversation has the power to expose to us the heart and thoughts of a person in a way that their speeches or articles seldom can.

Of course what is true of twentieth-century celebrities is

equally true of great men of the past. And it is true of a man
like Jesus. If we are really going to get to know Jesus, we
need to sample not just his formal teaching but his private
discussions too. We have to see him not only interacting
with the crowds, but also in more relaxed, one-to-one, personal encounters. He will always be a distant, even remote
figure to us—unless by some means we can listen in on his
conversations. And that, it seems to me, is the great bonus
of the gospel of John. Of course, Matthew, Mark and Luke
each have their distinctive contribution to make towards an
understanding of Jesus, which stem from each author's special interests and target audience. But the image that those
three gospels present to us is by and large shaped by the
public ministry of Jesus. They have that in common: the
stories he told, the miracles he performed, the teaching he
gave, as these stories and incidents were deliberately committed to memory by his disciples and passed down, often
in quite rigid oral traditions. And the result is that
Matthew, Mark and Luke all paint a remarkably similar
picture of Jesus. That is why scholars sometimes call them
the 'synoptic' gospels, from the Greek word which means
'viewed together'. They all look at Jesus, broadly speaking,
from the same angle. But not so John.

You only have to read a few verses of John to realise that
this gospel stands on its own. To start with, much of his
material is unique to his account. And even that material
which does find parallels in the other gospels is told in such
a different manner that it's impossible to determine
whether John used them as sources for his information or
not. Every word of John's gospel bears the hallmark of his
own distinctive style. Sceptics, of course, have not been
slow to interpret this divergence from the other gospels to
mean that this book is a work of pious fiction. According to
them, John was a second-century Christian philosopher
writing theology in the guise of history. But there is no concrete evidence to support that view. In fact, recent scholar-

ship has increasingly confirmed the gospel's historical accuracy, its Palestinian origins, even its early date.

The easiest way, in fact, to understand the difference between John's gospel and the other gospels is to compare it to the difference between a chat show and the nine o'clock news. John has not been content merely to compile and edit a collection of biographical snippets from Jesus' public life handed down from others. He wants us to meet Jesus in a far more intimate way than that, and that means through conversation. He wants us to hear Jesus talking. Accordingly he makes no attempt to chronicle everything about Jesus that he knew. Instead he selects from his memory just a handful of events and records those in very great detail.

The whole gospel is structured around just seven miracles. The other gospel writers would think little of including that many miracles in a single chapter. But John is not embarrassed by the paucity of his events because he is not interested in reproducing Jesus' diary. He is interested in painting Jesus' portrait. So he uses these seven miracles, or 'signs', as the narrative pegs on which to support seven great discourses—seven conversations, if you like, which expose to us the heart of Jesus, and how he understood himself. The result is similar to that of a television chat show; we feel we get to know Jesus through reading John in a way that the other gospels never quite achieve.

John takes us behind the public image to discover the inner personality of Jesus. And the remarkable thing is that the person you discover in that much more intimate setting is not only much more human than the synoptic news-reels might convey, he is also much more divine; he is not only easier to love, he is also much more compelling to worship.

In the course of this book we are going to be studying these seven great discourses in John's gospel. My hope is that as we do so, we will feel that we have been watching a chat show between Jesus and an expert interviewer. That is why I have called the book *Introducing Jesus.* And our first study, in John 3, is very typical of the kind of conversation we are going to be listening in on.

> There was a man of the Pharisees named Nicodemus, a member of the Jewish ruling council. He came to Jesus at night and said, 'Rabbi, we know you are a teacher who has come from God. For no-one could perform the miraculous signs you are doing if God were not with him' (3:1–2).

Here is just the sort of man we have been talking about; someone who was looking for the kind of personal chat with Jesus in which John is so interested. He had witnessed Jesus' public ministry, and he had been impressed. He had realised that this was no ordinary Jewish rabbi, but he wanted to know Jesus better, and that meant getting behind the media image somehow. So he sought a private inter-view.

John tells us he came by night. Some suggest that that was because Nicodemus, being an important man in Jewish society, did not want everybody to know that he was interested in Jesus. Others, more kindly perhaps, argue that it was simply the only way he could find of getting Jesus on his own for the kind of serious and unhurried conversa-tion that he wanted to have with him. We do not really know what his motivation was. But for myself, I strongly suspect that the main reason John records the lateness of the hour is that he sees a symbolic significance in it. Nicodemus not only met Jesus by night, but when he did so, he was in a very real sense a man living in the darkness. And the question his conversation ultimately revolves around is: did he love that darkness—or was he the kind of man who was willing to come to the light?

Let us look at the conversation together.

A vital experience (verses 3–8)

> I tell you the truth, unless a man is born again, he cannot see
> the kingdom of God (3:3).

It's a characteristic of human beings like ourselves that
we are always searching for something. Some of us interpret that 'something' in political terms; a just society, a better world. Others express it in more personal, religious or
philosophical terms. We are looking for a sense of fulfilment, a meaning to life's existence.

For the Jews in Jesus' day, these perennial human aspirations were all bound up with what they called 'the kingdom
of God'. Like us, some of them saw it politically, a coming
day when they would be emancipated from imperialism,
and their national independence restored under the rule of
God's Messiah. But others put more stress on the personal,
religious side of things. The kingdom of God for them
meant the achievement of moral perfection through obedience to God's law.

Nicodemus would probably have expounded the phrase
'the kingdom of God' in both ways, because he was a
Pharisee. It was the distinctive vocation of the Pharisees to
prepare the way (as they saw it) for the political kingdom of
God by their personal dedication to the religious kingdom
of God. As one scholar puts it: 'The Pharisees tried by
obedience to the law to be the true people of God preparing
the way for the Messiah.'

We know, both from other parts of the New Testament
and from first-century Jewish writings, that Nicodemus
would have been a man of very high moral standards and
almost fanatical spiritual commitment. He would have
been a strict sabbatarian for a start—no watching televised
sport on Sunday afternoon for him! He would have been
punctilious in his attendance at church and generous—in a
legalistic kind of way—to the poor. In his dress he would
have been a bit old-fashioned, even to the point of eccen-

tricity. But perhaps it would be in his attitude to the Bible that he would interest us most. Nicodemus would have been an extreme fundamentalist, reverencing not just every word of the sacred text, but every letter of it.

In other words, Nicodemus would in many ways have been what we would call 'Christian'. I suspect that is what most people meeting him today would think him to be. He believed that the key to a better world was a return to the Ten Commandments, and he confidently expected a coming day of judgement when God would send to hell those pagan advocates of permissiveness that thought otherwise.

So here is a fascinating encounter—Jesus meeting a 'Christian'. Perhaps we would expect Jesus to pat Nicodemus on the back, congratulate him for his theological conservatism, applaud his moral zeal and welcome him as an ally in their joint campaign to build the kingdom of God. But the surprise is that in point of fact Jesus' response to Nicodemus is quite different from that. Jesus very gently, but very firmly, draws a complete line of separation between the two of them. 'Nicodemus,' he says, 'you must be born again—yes, you and your Pharisee friends.' In fact, without such a regenerating experience, says Jesus, not only can you not enter this kingdom of God that you are searching for; you can not understand what it is, nor even see it. Everybody must be born again.

With that phrase Jesus separates himself not just from the Pharisees but from every ideology, every philosophy and every religion that the world can offer. The answer to our deepest human quest, he says, cannot be found by human effort, be it political revolutions or religious disciplines. Utopia is never going to arrive however much you campaign for justice. Perfection will never be achieved for all your moral zeal.

You must be born again, he says. For evil is not some learned response. It is not some product of our social conditioning, but an intrinsic component of our genetic make-up. It is an incorrigible tendency inside us to self-centredness and to pride, and it perpetually frustrates our best attempts to make either ourselves or our world a better place. No amount of social reorganisation, no amount of education, no amount of self-discipline can ever eliminate that fundamental moral perversion in the human heart.

How mistaken, then, are those people who equate Christianity with conservatism! Jesus is revealed in these verses to be one of the most radical thinkers the world has ever seen. According to him, the trouble with the Marxists is not that they are revolutionary, but that they are not half revolutionary enough! Man does not just need a new economic order, he needs a new birth. No wonder Nicodemus is flabbergasted. 'Born again, Jesus? Born again, me? But that's impossible!'

> How can a man be born when he is old? . . . Surely he cannot enter a second time into his mother's womb to be born? (3:4).

To be fair to Nicodemus, it is most unlikely that a man of his education would have misunderstood Jesus in the crudely literalistic way that his reply might suggest. I doubt very much whether Nicodemus seriously imagined that Jesus was suggesting a physical return to the womb.

No, Nicodemus was wise enough to realise that the adult human personality is not something you can change easily, if at all. He didn't need the insights of modern biochemistry and psychiatry to tell him that every individual is the product of his past—his parents' genes, his foetal trauma, his infantile parenting, his childhood experiences, his adolescent crises, his habits, his decisions, his relationships. Every man is constructed out of these influences on his personality. John Clare the poet once wrote: 'If life had a second edition, how I would correct the proofs!' But by an unchangeable policy of the publishing house, we are never given that opportunity. Much as we might cry with Tennyson 'Ah for a man to arise in me, that the man I am may cease to be,' it cannot be so. We can never turn the clock back to rediscover our intra-uterine innocence. That, says Nicodemus, lies outside the range of possibility. It cannot be done. Not so, replies Jesus. It may lie outside the range of human possibility, but it does not lie outside the range of divine possibility.

> I tell you the truth, unless a man is born of water and the Spirit, he cannot enter the kingdom of God. Flesh gives birth to flesh, but the Spirit gives birth to spirit. You should not be surprised at my saying, 'You must be born again' (3:5–7).

There has been a good deal of debate about precisely what that word 'water' means. Some take it to be a reference to natural birth—perhaps the waters in which a baby lies in the womb, or even the male seed from which it is conceived. That would obviously follow on from what Nicodemus said earlier. Jesus would be saying that unless a man supplements the physical birth which Nicodemus is talking about, with the spiritual birth which he is talking about, he cannot enter the kingdom of God. But it has to be admitted that water is a very strange way of talking about natural birth, and one would have thought that Jesus would have found less obscure terminology.

A second, perhaps more likely, suggestion is that the word 'water' is symbolic. Water, as we will see in the next chapter, is often used in John's gospel as a picture of the spiritual life Jesus comes to bring. In fact in a very important Old Testament reference, the prophet Ezekiel speaks of the kingdom of God as a time when God's people will be washed with water and indwelt by the Spirit (cf. Ezek 36:25–27). If that verse with its symbolism is in the back of his mind, then Jesus is saying that unless a person is born again from that spiritual fountain of cleansing and renewal of which the prophet speaks, he cannot enter the kingdom of God. But again, that does seem to be reading rather a lot into a few words.

Undoubtedly the commonest interpretation of the word 'water' takes it to be an allusion to baptism. It is certainly very difficult to believe that John's Christian readers would not see such an application, knowing as they did that Christian baptism was a dramatic pictorial representation of precisely this new birth that Jesus is talking about. But though John may have intended us to catch that overtone in the words, I think that it can hardly have been the primary meaning of the word as Jesus originally spoke it, since Nicodemus was not a Christian and could not be expected to understand Christian baptism as John's later readers did.

If the word 'water' does refer to baptism, I think it must be a reference to the baptism of John the Baptist. If you look back to verse 33 of chapter 1, you will see there a key verse in which John the Baptist draws a distinction between his watery baptism and the baptism of the Holy Spirit which would be Jesus' unique prerogative. And if that is the context in which we are to understand it, then what Jesus is really saying here is this: 'John's waters of repentance aren't enough, you need the spirit of regeneration too, if you are to enter the kingdom of heaven.'

It is difficult to choose between all these possibilities, though for myself I think that the last one is probably the most likely. It would be quite like John, of course, to have all these meanings to some extent in mind and to have left the ambiguity there intentionally in order to generate as many reverberations in his readers' minds as possible. Suffice it to say, that 'water', whatever it precisely means, is not the most important word in verse 5. The most important word is 'spirit'. Jesus makes that very plain in the next verse.

Flesh gives birth to flesh, but the Spirit gives birth to spirit (3:6).

In plain words, what Jesus is getting at here is that this new birth he describes is miraculous. There is no way human nature can evolve into the life of the kingdom of God naturally. There is a qualitative discontinuity, separating sinful humanity from the fulfilment of its highest aspirations. But the Spirit of God, says Jesus, has the creative power to perform the inner transformation needed to enable a person to make that quantum leap into a new world. Yes, the new birth may be supernatural, but not impossible. And to prove it he gives an illustration.

> The wind blows wherever it pleases. You hear its sound, but you cannot tell where it comes from or where it is going. So it is with everyone born of the Spirit (3:8).

The point here is that the word in Greek and Hebrew for wind is the same as the word for Spirit. So Jesus is making a kind of elaborate pun. Nicodemus cannot believe this new birth business; he finds it too incomprehensible. Jesus replies, 'You understand the wind, don't you? No, of course you don't. But you believe in it readily enough. Well, there is something profoundly mysterious about the new birth too. Like the wind, God's Spirit moves sovereignly among the human race. You cannot control him, you cannot predict his next move or fathom the laws of his operation. In that sense, he is rightly called the wind. All you can do is observe the effects of his intervention in people's lives—his sound. And those effects are real. As real as the havoc wrought by a typhoon such as those we see on TV news.

A little boy once asked a sailor on the quay, 'What is the wind?'

'The wind?' replied the sailor, 'I don't rightly know what the wind is; but I can hoist a sail.' That's pretty much what Jesus is saying to Nicodemus. You do not have to know *how* the Spirit creates new life in people. It is miraculous, mysterious. No psychiatrist will ever explain it. No theologian will ever fully formulate it. But you can *experience* it! You can hoist a sail.

This is why Jesus says that we should not be surprised at his phrase 'you must be born again'. Notice carefully that word 'must'. Jesus does not say 'may'. This is not a spiritual extra for the specially religious. It is a spiritual necessity. The story is told that George Whitefield's sponsor, the Countess of Huntingdon, once asked him why he was always preaching on John 3:5: 'You must be born again.' Whitefield replied, 'Madam, because you *must*.' It is as simple as that. In the most literal sense of that word, this is a *vital* experience, a matter of life or death.

Perhaps some of you reading this are like Nicodemus, pillars of the establishment: scholars, academics, religious people. Jesus says to you, 'You must be born again!' Perhaps some of you are as different from Nicodemus as chalk from cheese: uneducated, with no academic pretensions, irreligious people even, with no claims to moral excellence such as Nicodemus had. But Jesus says the same to you. 'You must be born again!' For unless we are born again, we are never going to find the answer to that inner restlessness that drives us on in search of a better world and a fuller life. Unless a man is born again, says Jesus, he cannot see the kingdom of God.

A unique Person (verses 9–17)

'How can this be?' Nicodemus asked.

'You are Israel's teacher,' said Jesus, 'and do you not understand these things? I tell you the truth, we speak of what we know, and we testify to what we have seen, but still you people do not accept our testimony' (3:9–11).

Nicodemus thought his problem was that he couldn't understand Jesus' teaching. What Jesus is leading him to realise here is that that was not really his problem at all. His real problem was that he had an inadequate estimate of the person to whom he was talking. In fact that had been his problem right from the beginning of the conversation. Consider his opening remarks. He came to Jesus and said, 'Rabbi, we know you are a teacher who has come from God.' A flattering remark, of course; but also a trifle condescending. '*We* know.' To whom does he refer by that 'we'? I suppose to himself and to all his pharisaical cronies. 'Yes, Jesus,' Nicodemus is saying, 'we of the Jewish elite have been quite impressed by your performance, you know. We are disposed to think you are a teacher come from God.' Big deal! Frankly, that's a little bit like the fourth-form G.C.S.E. maths set complimenting Albert Einstein on his arithmetic.

Jesus was certainly a teacher come from God, but not at all in the way Nicodemus thought! And it is quite clear that one of the reasons Jesus embarked on this mystifying discussion of the new birth was precisely to bring this patronising Pharisee down a peg or two. 'You're *the* teacher of Israel aren't you? At least you pretend to be. You are on the selection committee. You decide who the faculty are going to be. You are the one who tells people who is "a teacher come from God" and who is not. Then surely *you* know about these things.' Can you not hear the gentle mockery in his tone as he echoes that first person plural with which Nicodemus had introduced himself? '*We* speak of what *we* know,' says Jesus. '*We* testify to what *we*'ve seen. Your problem, Nicodemus, is not that you cannot understand what I'm saying, but that you do not think sufficiently highly of me yet to believe that I know what I am talking about.'

When Jesus speaks to us about the things of God, he is not offering us the speculations of a philosopher, nor the expositions of a preacher, nor even the inspirations of a prophet. He's offering us first-hand knowledge, divine revelation of a quite unique kind: 'We testify to what we

have seen.' That being so, it is not our ability to understand
that is the real crux, but our willingness to believe.

> I have spoken to you of earthly things and you do not believe;
> how then will you believe if I speak of heavenly things? (3:12).

It is not totally clear what Jesus means by 'earthly things'.
But probably he is referring to the analogy he has just
drawn between the Spirit and the wind, which proved so
perplexing to Nicodemus.

'You do not take my word for it Nicodemus,' Jesus is saying, 'even when I use the language of material things to
explain it to you. But there are many aspects of the revelation that I bring for which no earthly analogy is available.
They pertain wholly to heavenly realities that defy com-
parison to anything you have ever experienced,
Nicodemus. If you cannot trust me when I tell you about
the way of the wind, how ever will you trust me when I tell
you about the way of salvation?

> No-one has ever gone into heaven except the one who came
> from heaven—the Son of Man. Just as Moses lifted up the
> snake in the desert, so the Son of Man must be lifted up, that
> everyone who believes may have eternal life in him. For God so
> loved the world that he gave his one and only Son, that whoever
> believes in him shall not perish but have eternal life (3:13–16).

These are among the most famous words in the whole
Bible. Just observe what these verses have to teach us about
the uniqueness of Jesus. Notice his titles: 'the Son of Man',
'the one who came down from heaven', 'The one and only
Son of God'. Notice too his mission. 'God did not send his
Son into the world to condemn the world, but to save it.' No
other man who has ever walked this earth has claimed an
identity or a mission so stupendous. To a Jew like
Nicodemus, who understood far more of the background of
titles like the Son of Man and the Son of God than we do,

these words were blasphemous, heretical and outrageously
ridiculous. It is little surprise that we do not find him speaking again. A stupefied silence was about all one could
expect after such a mind-blowing exposition of Jesus' self-
understanding.

There is no possible way, of course, that claims like these
can be scientifically verified. There is no experiment that
you can perform in order to prove that these verses are
true. These are 'heavenly things'. Such things can only be
known by revelation and can only be appropriated by faith.
But is faith really such a difficult thing? Nicodemus seems
to have found it so.

But Jesus perhaps implies that he should not have done.
He reminds him of an incident in the Old Testament when
the Israelites were in the wilderness. The people were
rebelling against God and a plague of poisonous snakes was
sent into their camp to chasten them. In their desperation,
Moses tells us, they confessed their sin and cried to him to
provide some remedy for the venom. And Moses was told
to make a bronze snake and put it on a pole; and any Israel-
ite who looked at that snake would be healed (cf. Num
21:4–9).

It's a puzzling story in lots of ways. Making an animal
image like that seems a very uncharacteristic thing for God
to tell Moses to do. Some of those Israelites may have
looked at it with a gaze bordering on superstition or even
idolatry. They certainly cannot have understood how a
bronze replica of a snake could take the bite of the real
thing away. They simply had to take Moses' word for it and
believe. They had no other choice.

Jesus is saying here that it is the same for us and for
Nicodemus. 'One day soon, Nicodemus,' he explains, 'you
will see me lifted up on a pole, arms outstretched, just like
that snake in the desert. You will not be able to understand
that, any more than the Israelites could understand the
snake. Nobody will, not fully. But, Nicodemus, if only *you*

can trust me! Trust me enough to believe that I know what I'm talking about, that I know what I'm doing. For I tell you this, Nicodemus, every man and woman who looks up at me on that ignominious stake, feeling their need of salvation, conscious of their failure, knowing they need the mercy of God to deliver them, is going to find rescue in that look of faith. More than that, they are going to find the life of the age to come—the new life of that kingdom of God that we have been talking about. Do you not see, Nicodemus, that you are asking the wrong question? The right question is not '*How* can this be?' The question you should be asking as you stand there looking at me is '*Who* can this be?'

That's the question you too have to ask as you read this. All too often you find people like Nicodemus who dabble wistfully on the margins of Christian commitment. And all too often, their arguments are the same. 'Oh, I can't believe a loving God would send people to hell' . . . 'I can't believe in substitutionary atonement' . . . 'I can't believe in predestination' . . . 'I can't believe in the inspiration of the Bible' . . . 'I can't believe this, I can't accept that.'

Do you know what they are? They are all subspecies of the genus Nicodemus! 'How can this be?' they ask. 'If only I could believe this or that doctrine I might be able to follow Christ. But I have my intellectual doubts, you know. They preclude the possibility.' If that is what you are saying, you are fooling yourself. It does not work like that. Christianity is not the intellectual acceptance of a set of theological propositions which you have managed to convince yourself of by rational demonstrations. Christianity is a response of personal trust, directed towards Jesus himself.

Of course you will have intellectual problems. I have had intellectual problems ever since I became a Christian, and I expect I shall have them until I die and faith turns into sight. It is not our theological problems that hinder us from finding faith, any more than it was for Nicodemus. It is our unwillingness to surrender our mind and heart to the authority of Jesus. And that brings us to the final part of the conversation.

A critical verdict (verses 18–21)

> Whoever believes in him is not condemned, but whoever does not believe stands condemned already because he has not believed in the name of God's one and only Son (3:18).

The curator of an art gallery was immensely proud of his collection of fine paintings, but he was rather intolerant of the cultural philistines who sometimes came to view them. One day as he was walking through the gallery he heard a tourist comment, 'Oh what a dreadful picture! I can't understand why they should hang such a monstrosity in public.' Incensed, the curator stepped forward, and turning to the visitor, he said, 'Sir, the merit of these paintings is not in question. It is those who view them who are on trial!' It's a good point. Sometimes our verdicts judge us more than they judge others.

And that, according to Jesus, is certainly true of our verdict upon him. 'Human destiny,' he says, 'is ultimately sealed by how people respond to me.' With a single exception, God will forgive a person absolutely anything. Whatever is on your conscience today, God will forgive it. He loves the world, and does not want it to perish. He gave his one and only Son that it might not perish.

There is only one thing that he will never forgive. And that is the blindness, the arrogance, the downright ingratitude of those who reject that gift.

> This is the verdict: Light has come into the world, but men loved darkness instead of light because their deeds were evil. Everyone who does evil hates the light, and will not come into the light for fear that his deeds will be exposed. But whoever

lives by the truth comes into the light, so that it may be seen plainly that what he has done has been done through God (3:19–21).

Some of you reading this are not Christians. May I ask you why? Will you tell me, 'Well, I'm looking for the answer to one of those intellectual problems you wrote about earlier?' Will you tell me that you are waiting to be zapped by some spiritual experience that will blow your mind? Will you tell me that you are too busy to consider it, postponing it until some later day when you have more leisure? Will you tell me that you are simply indifferent to it, unable to feel that this Christianity business is really your scene?

I would not wish to criticise the sincerity of your reasons for being an unbeliever. I would not be so rude. But Jesus would. He is rude enough to question your excuses, and he does so right here. Jesus, in these closing verses of his conversation with Nicodemus, says that all such excuses are really just a smoke-screen, a tissue of self-deception. Jesus insists that the real reason you do not believe in him today is not your intellectual problems, not your lack of spiritual experiences, not your busyness, not your indifference. The real reason, he says, is your sin.

People do not want to become Christians for one reason and one reason only, and that is because they know it will mean moral change. And they do not want to change. Deep down at the deepest level of our personal honesty we know who he is, and we know that he is telling the truth. Our problem is that we are not willing to live by that truth. We would rather sacrifice our integrity than lose our pride. We would rather stay in the dark, says Jesus, than move into the light and admit what we are really like. Jesus insists that our excuses do not hold water. Our spiritual blindness, he asserts, is a culpable blindness. It is not that we cannot see the light. It is that we *will* not see it. This is the verdict. Light has come into the world but men love darkness.

I wonder how long Nicodemus chatted to Jesus. Obviously, John has only given us a resumé of their conversation. I expect it went on for much longer. Could it be that they talked all night? It would not surprise me if they did. Nicodemus arrived in the dark. Perhaps as he left, the first glimmerings of dawn were hovering on the horizon? And did he smile, I wonder, at that rising sun—or turn his back upon it, glueing his eyes to his own shadow? Such a choice confronts us, does it not? We have seen what Jesus had to say about this *vital experience*: 'You must be born again.' We have seen what he has to say about *his own uniqueness*: 'God sent the Son into the world to save the world.' Now, he insists, a *verdict* will be given. He is not asking that we understand everything he has said in this conversation. Nobody can do that. The greatest theologian cannot do that. He is asking simply that we believe in him.

2

The Empty Life

John 4:1–28

Life, said the critic James Huneker, is like an onion. You peel off layer after layer, only to discover at the end that there is nothing in it—nothing except tears, perhaps. I think that the woman of Samaria would have agreed with that sentiment. It is not difficult from the little bit we are told about her to imagine the kind of person she was. Like most of us, she was looking for happiness.

But unfortunately happiness kept on eluding her grasp. The current man in her life, we are told, was number six. Some advocates of the permissive society would no doubt hail this as a testimony to the unfettered joy of sexual liberation. But I am pretty sure she did not see it that way.

She had hoped, like many, that love and marriage would make her life worthwhile, giving it meaning, and direction. But somehow every relationship had turned sour on her. Each time she had found a new man she had thought at last this is it, her Mr Right. She hoped she would not make the same mistake again. But she did. And the more emotional tragedy she experienced, the more onion-like her life became. Already the romantic idealism of her youth had hardened into a frustrated cynicism about things.

And as for the future, well, that did not bear thinking about. Age would steal her beauty. Her men friends would turn to younger sport. There would be little left for her

except the gutter. She could see herself in it now. A loath-
some old piece of laced mutton pathetically courting the
favours of any man drunk enough or desperate enough to
want her. If the truth were known she was already half-way
there. Her self-respect was in tatters. Why else would she
choose to come to this isolated travellers' well at the hottest
time of the day, except to avoid the embarrassment of being
shunned by all those respectable neighbours of hers?

She would give anything to relieve the depression that
haunted her. She felt so insecure, so lonely. But most of all
she felt so dissatisfied. 'In the small hours,' wrote Cyril
Connolly, 'when the acrid stench of existence rises like
sewer gas from everything created, the emptiness of life
seems more terrible than its misery.' Yes, this woman knew
about those small hours that Connolly speaks about, those
sleepless nights born not of overwork, but simply of the
unrelenting futility of it all.

Take the wretched water pot she had carried from the village for instance. There it stood, empty again. She had filled it yesterday. She would fill it again tomorrow. It was
like her life—a symbol of never-ending thirst. She would
spend the remainder of her days filling that pot and at the
end its appetite would be as insatiable as ever. I do not
know if you have ever had one of those days when you felt
so irritated that you wanted to smash a perfectly innocent
piece of pottery against the wall. But I suspect that this
woman sometimes felt like that about her water pot.
Empty. Empty again. That was her water pot and that was
her.

Is that how you often feel? Kirk Douglas, the Hollywood
actor, once likened his life to the script of a second-feature
movie. 'It was that corny,' he said. 'If someone offered me
the screenplay of my life to film I'd turn it down flat.' There
are millions of people with lives far less exciting than Kirk
Douglas' who would say something similar. They are
bored—bored out of their minds by the sheer tedium of

existence. Like a rat trapped in an insoluble maze, or like a wheel caught in a never-ending rut, they long for something to shatter the monotony, to fill the vacuum.

But the irony is that they do not even know what it is that they really want, let alone where to find it. They try another job. They try another marriage. They try alcohol. They try drugs. They try the ersatz thrill of the latest fantasy movie. They try the hypnotic stupor of the TV screen. They try the pools coupon, the holiday brochure, the Mills and Boon romance. But none of it works. At best these things offer no more than temporary escape. Those sleepless small hours always return, and with them the emptiness.

No, we do not really need John to spell out what the woman of Samaria felt about life, do we? For she is a woman in whose face we can see mirrored the inner anguish of millions, who daily peel off the layers of their onion-like existence only to discover nothing. Nothing but tears. There may be some parts of John's gospel that we will find hard to relate to. But no one can say this woman is not relevant to the twentieth century. You can see a thousand like her within a square mile of where you live. And that being so, we would do well to consider her story very carefully. For our study tells us how one day, quite out of the blue, quite unexpectedly, this empty woman met Someone who in the space of a single conversation transformed her emptiness into a sparkling fountain of satisfaction and joy. That is the second conversation which John recounts to us, because he is convinced that that Someone can do the same for us.

A question of curiosity

[Jesus] had to go through Samaria. So he came to a town in Samaria called Sychar . . . . [and] tired as he was from the journey, sat down by the well. It was about the sixth hour. When a Samaritan woman came to draw water, Jesus said to her, 'Will you give me a drink?' (4:4–7).

It is interesting that John starts off by saying that Jesus *had* to go through Samaria, because the fact is there was no necessity about it at all, humanly speaking. Pious Jews avoided that particular route like the plague, preferring to go several miles out of their way rather than risk social intercourse with the despised Samaritans. If Jesus had been in some particular hurry, his breach of normal practice might have been understandable. But there is no evidence to suggest that his journey was a particularly urgent one— quite the opposite in fact. Verses 1–3 indicated that had it not been for some animosity in Jerusalem, Jesus would have stayed in Judea longer. He certainly is conscious of no pressing appointment in Galilee.

The only reason, then, for saying Jesus *had* to go through Samaria must be that an important encounter awaited him *en route*. It is, in other words, John's subtle way of telling us that this meeting with the woman of Samaria was no chance matter. It took place, like everything in Jesus' life, by divine arrangement. There was a 'must' about it. The woman had no idea about it of course, nor did Jesus give her any hint of it in his opening remark to her. Unlike some Christians who would leap heavily in with boorish questions such as 'Are you saved, sister?', Jesus is a model of tact and discretion. 'Will you give me a drink?' He gives no indication that there is going to be a religious element in this conversation at all. And yet the woman's interest is aroused by the remark.

You are a Jew and I am a Samaritan woman. How can you ask me for a drink? (4:9).

The reason for her surprise is simple. Jesus was flouting two deeply embedded social conventions of his day. Firstly, he was ignoring the hatred which had kept Jews and Samaritans in mutually exclusive communities for four centuries. As John puts it, 'Jews do not associate with Samaritans' (v.9), and that is putting it mildly. But secondly, Jesus was ignoring the gentlemanly decorum which forbade any respectable Middle-Eastern man from having a private exchange with a woman in public. The Rabbis held that it was even improper for a husband to talk to his wife in public. Whatever would they have thought about a man chatting to a woman of such mongrel pedigree and such low moral reputation as this! There can be little wonder, then, that the woman is taken aback by this strange Jew who wanted to engage her in conversation.

There is a moving lesson for us in that. Jesus is not bothered who you are, or what the world thinks of you. He is not hampered in his dealings with people by those discriminations which affect us so much, be they racist or sexist or any other. Maybe society has given us a low self-image, and told us, for example, that we are not worth much because we are black, or working-class, or even just because we are a woman. Jesus does not think like that. In the previous chapter we saw him talking to a male Jewish aristocrat, Nicodemus. Here he is talking to a female Samaritan peasant. The social contrast could not be more extreme. But Jesus speaks to both with equal concern, and with equal respect.

So whoever you are, you need have no fear that Jesus is not interested in you. On the contrary, he may well have brought you to read this just in order to meet with you. You have not realised it yet of course, any more than did this woman of Samaria. All you feel at present is a mild curiosity. You have met some Christians, maybe, and you have seen they are a little different. You have read a bit of the Bible and perhaps it seems strange. So you are reading this book. Well, be warned! For once you are in conversation with Jesus Christ, anything could happen. That is how it

began for this woman. She was a little intrigued. That is all.
But it did not stay like that for long!

A sense of need

> If you knew the gift of God and who it is that asks you for a
> drink, you would have asked him and he would have given you
> living water (4:10).

So the small-talk is quickly dispensed with. With the skill
of a master interviewer, Jesus breaks through the chit-chat
to challenge that spiritual emptiness in this woman's life. It
is hardly surprising that she is not really prepared to be
manoeuvred into a religious discussion of that sort quite so
easily.

> Sir, . . . you have nothing to draw with and the well is deep.
> Where can you get this living water? Are you greater than our
> father Jacob? (4:11–12).

Commentators differ about how we ought to take that
retort. Some think she has genuinely misunderstood Jesus.
She has taken his words about living water literally and
thinks he is offering to tell her about some hidden spring
nearby; and knowing the place as well as she does, she is
understandably sceptical.

Personally, I think that a rather unlikely explanation.
She was an intelligent woman. She knew that Jesus was
bantering with her, playing word-games. This is the sort of
woman who had been chatted up by quite enough men to
know when they were working some conversational angle.
She was not naive.

No, she had decided to play along with him. I suspect
there was a mischievous glint in her eye, perhaps even a
hint of flirtatiousness, as she retorts to what she took to be
Jesus' little jest with feigned indignation. 'Oh that's big'
talk, that is! Who do you think you are then? Tormenting a

poor working girl like me with offers of running water when
you haven't even got a bucket to help yourself to this stag-
nant pool you are sitting on! Obviously, water that was
good enough for the patriarchs isn't good enough for the
likes of you, is it?' But Jesus is not to be diverted from his
purpose so easily.

> Everyone who drinks this water will be thirsty again, but who-
> ever drinks the water I give him will never thirst. Indeed, the
> water I give him will become in him a spring of water welling up
> to eternal life. (4:13–14).

Have you ever been walking the hills and found yourself
in the middle of nowhere, with an empty flask and a long
way to go? Then suddenly you stumble on one of those little
ice-cold mountain streams that flow down from the rocks.
It is crystal-clear, sparkling, invigorating, refreshing—better than anything the City Water Board can provide.

That is what Jesus says he can give to men and women—
an inner fountain of bubbling vitality that satisfies a person's spiritual thirst, not just once but permanently. He is
saying, in other words, that he is the answer to the emptiness that gnaws our souls as it gnawed this woman's soul.
Life with him is no onion! It's a cascade of fulfilment and
joy, he says; and this time, the woman's reply is just a little
less dismissive.

> Sir, give me this water so that I won't get thirsty and have to
> keep coming here to draw water (4:15).

Once again, I strongly suspect that there is an element of
playfulness in her words. She is being sarcastic, urging him,
'Please give me some of this wonderful water, Sir. I can't
wait! Carting this water pot to and fro every day is driving
me slowly up the wall.'

But there is, at the very least, a certain wistfulness under-
lying her words, even if they are flippant. For all her

humour, Jesus has struck a serious chord in her heart. It is as if she is saying, 'It would be a very nice trick if you could do it, stranger. Would that you could wave your magic wand and free me from this cycle of drudgery to which I am victim.' And for Jesus, that invitation, half-joking though it may well have been, is enough. All he was after was some conscious confession on this woman's part of her sense of need.

The trouble with most of us is that we are not willing to make such a confession. We insist on pretending everything is OK, because, if the truth were known, we live a lot closer to despair than we can afford to admit. So we erect all kinds of defence mechanisms against anything that threatens to expose our inward spiritual poverty.

Lighthearted self-mockery is one of the most common. 'Me get religious? Oh yes, I can just fancy myself in a halo,' we say. But deep down beneath that tongue-in-the-cheek humour there is a real spiritual longing. We would not joke about it if it were not so.

If you are going to find Jesus' answer to that emptiness of which I have spoken, you have got to be willing to confess your need. Jesus once put it this way: 'People who are healthy do not need a doctor, only those who are sick.' What can the doctor do for the patient who refuses to admit he has a problem? So do not come to Doctor Jesus telling him that you are fine. If you do that, you will be completely unhelped. He will do you no good at all. You must be willing to admit that your life is empty, that you are longing for something to satisfy your spiritual thirst.

But if you say something like that to him he will be at your side in a moment. Once again, be warned! If you admit a need to Doctor Jesus, no matter how sardonically, you may well find he will prescribe surgery before he gets down to giving you the medicine you are after!

A stab of conscience

> He told her, 'Go call your husband and come back.' 'I have no husband,' she replied. Jesus said to her, 'You are right when you say you have no husband. The fact is, you have had five husbands, and the man you now have is not your husband. What you have just said is quite true' (4:16–18).

So Jesus can be sarcastic too when he wants to be! Why does he suddenly introduce this sordid dimension into the conversation? Surely this woman's love life is her own concern. All Jesus is doing by such an unwarranted intrusion into her private affairs is to risk her storming off in fury, with all kinds of 'How dare you' and 'I don't have to put up with this!' falling on the ear. Until now, Jesus has been a model of discretion. Why does he suddenly display such uncharacteristic tactlessness?

The answer, of course, is that he has to; and not just in the case of this Samaritan woman, but in that of all of us. We assume that the root of our emptiness is boredom. 'If my life were more interesting,' we say, 'it would be all right. If only I could find the right job. If only I could find the right marriage partner. Then my feelings of frustration and dissatisfaction with life would all evaporate.' Countless thousands of people say that to themselves. But it is not so. Our real problem is not with our jobs, or with our marriages. Our real problem is with ourselves.

Our emptiness is at root not circumstantial in origin—it is moral. We human beings were made by God with certain behavioural norms in mind and we have deliberately flouted them. We have rebelled against God's rules for our lives like disobedient children kicking against their parents' authority. And God has locked us in the bedroom to teach us a lesson. We feel bored up there. We feel empty inside. For we were designed to share the life of God with him. But our foolish insistence on our own way has severed that relationship and the water of life that flows from it, leaving us lonely, insecure, and directionless. We are at odds with ourselves, at odds with one another, at odds even with the universe.

And what do we do in response? Why, we spend all our days trying to plug that gap which God's absence has left. As often as not these days we try to plug it, as this woman did, with sexual adventure. But it never works. For no human relationship, no matter how emotionally intense, can be a substitute for the relationship with God that we were made for. No, before Jesus can meet our need, he has to show us the diagnosis. And the diagnosis is our moral failure. It is always a painful experience to have that exposed to us.

There is a story told of a Mexican who was arrested outside a police station while admiring his own photograph on the 'wanted' poster. Most of us, however, find guilt something we would far rather not face up to. It is certainly not something we admire in ourselves; rather it makes us feel ashamed, and embarrassed. But Jesus insists that it is not enough just to admit that you have a sense of need. You must also be willing to admit a sense of sin. No answers can be found until surgery has exposed that inner moral cancer.

We all have our skeletons in the cupboard. We all have things in our lives that we cannot remember without embarrassment. We all have thoughts lurking in our imaginations that would make us blush if they were displayed for public view.

But such is our pride that most of us engage in a kind of inner psychological conspiracy to conceal that secret shame. We think we are safe. We can pretend we are good people. We can even believe that lie ourselves. But I have to tell you that is not true. Jesus sees through our subterfuge. Our lives are transparent to his gaze. He sees those deeds and thoughts as clearly as he saw this woman's six love affairs. And he insists that we see them too, that we build this new kind of life he wants to give us on the humiliating self-knowledge that we are moral failures, spiritual bankrupts, sinners. He will not let us get away with anything less than that. For the water of life that we are looking for is the gift of God and God gives it, by a policy to which he strictly adheres, to penitents only.

A response of heart

> I can see that you are a prophet. Our fathers worshipped on this mountain, but you Jews claim that the place where we must worship is in Jerusalem (4:19–20).

Now most commentators interpret this as a red herring thrown into the conversation by the woman in a desperate attempt to change the subject. And I am sure that, in measure, that is exactly what it was. Nobody likes talking about their sin longer than they have to. Theology is a much less threatening subject, and provides abundant red herrings with which to divert attention from more personal issues. 'What about the pagans?' . . . 'What about other religions?' . . . 'What about all these Christian denominations?' It is all the same thing—'Jerusalem or Samaria?' And usually it is no more than a smoke-screen, with which people try to avoid the moral challenge of the Bible.

But to give this woman her due, I feel that in her case it was more than that. Jesus' exposé of her immoral lifestyle had gone home, and she may well have been grateful to get off the subject of her previous husbands, but the question she raises here was not necessarily a mere ploy.

She had suddenly realised that this man, whom she had taken for a rather liberal-minded Jew, was nothing less than a prophet with supernatural knowledge of her sin. She knew enough about religion to realise that in such an encounter she was being summoned to get right with God. The obvious question for a woman with her particular background was, where could she do so? 'You point at my sin, you tell me my life is wrong. Where do I compensate for

that? Where do I offer sacrifice in order to make it right? At
the temple in Jerusalem, or one in Samaria?' It may have
been partly a red herring, but it was also a very valid question.

The multitude of world religions can be a mere diversio-
nary tactic but it can also be a genuine intellectual problem
for people. It does need an answer, and Jesus graciously
gives her one.

> Believe me, woman, a time is coming when you will worship
> the Father neither on this mountain nor in Jerusalem. You
> Samaritans worship what you do not know; we worship what
> we do know, for salvation is from the Jews. Yet a time is com-
> ing and has now come when the true worshippers will worship
> the Father in spirit and truth, for they are the kind of worship-
> pers the Father seeks. God is Spirit, and his worshippers must
> worship in spirit and in truth (4:21–24).

These words express some very important things about
the nature of Christianity. Notice first what Jesus does *not*
say. He does not say what our hyper-tolerant pluralist
twentieth-century world would very much want him to
say—namely that all religions are true. We would like him
to mouth comforting platitudes about the difference
between Jews and Samaritans being superficial and historical. We would prefer him to praise Samaritan religion and
to urge that Samaritans were already finding God in their
own way, to echo Gandhi's opinion that 'the soul of all
religions is one' and it is only in outward form that they differ.

But Jesus says nothing of the kind. On the contrary, if
you look carefully, you will see here that Jesus insists upon
the unique religious privilege of the Jewish people as the
historical focus both of divine revelation and divine
redemption. They worshipped on the basis of knowledge;
the Samaritans on the basis of ignorance. If that was embar-
rassing or offensive to this woman's Samaritan pride, Jesus

does not spare it. God has chosen to make the Jewish people the vehicle of his plan of salvation. As a result nobody is ever going to find spiritual emancipation in this world unless they have dealings with Jewish culture. For deliverance from sin is something which God has accomplished inescapably in a context of Jewish history. Jesus insists that that is the way it is. If we are disposed to call it unfair, he might reply that the Jews have paid for their privilege many times over the centuries.

It is most important that we understand this. There is a tendency these days to bathe in nationalistic sentiment. The last night of the Proms shows that the British are still capable of it. 'God who made thee mighty, make thee mightier yet,' we sing. Go to Africa, Asia, or America, and you find the same kind of jingoistic pride. We will not accept that we are indebted to any other culture than our own. But it is not true! Each one of us, whichever culture we come from, depends on the Jewish people for our knowledge of God. Jesus makes that abundantly clear, and we have no choice but to swallow it.

But I want you to notice too that Jesus goes beyond that in his reply to the woman's question. 'Believe me,' he says to her, 'you stand on the threshold of a new era. A new hour is coming—and yes, it has already come.' And one of the characteristics of it is that access to God is no longer tied to any one culture as it was in the past. The historical privileges of the Jews are on the point of becoming obsolete and irrelevant. It will soon be neither a matter of Jerusalem nor Samaria. In the new era of God's kingdom, it is going to be a matter of spirit and truth.

Now we need to be very careful in interpreting what Jesus means by those enigmatic words. It is often said, of course, that what Jesus is teaching here is that God is non-material, that is he is not localised in any particular place. So the vital issue is not *where* you worship but *how* you worship, namely in sincerity of heart. And that is true up to a point; the words, 'spirit and truth', undoubtedly do emphasise that true worship is not a matter of mere form. However, if we said no more than that, we could be excused for thinking that Jesus is endorsing precisely the kind of liberal universalism that is so appealing to twentieth-century man. 'It does not matter what you believe, so long as you are sincere.'

But that would be to misunderstand completely what Jesus is trying to establish. The fact is that heart attitude has always been important to true worship. That is nothing new. God has always despised cant and hypocrisy. He has never been satisfied with mere religious formality. 'The sacrifices of God,' says David, 'are . . . a broken and contrite heart' (Ps 51:17); 'Rend your heart and not your garments,' says another prophet (Joel 2:13). There is nothing novel in such thoughts. And yet Jesus is speaking quite distinctly here about a radical change in the way in which men and women relate to God. A new hour.

Clearly, then, spirit and truth cannot just be mere synonyms for sincerity. There must be something more to it than that. And there is! If you study John's gospel as a whole, you will discover that 'spirit and truth' are key words in his vocabulary. And they are not trite or trivial in their meaning. They are far-reaching, and very profound. The vital thing about these words when John uses them is that they are very closely bound up with the person and ministry of Jesus himself.

When John speaks of 'Spirit' he is not merely emphasising that God is non-material, but that the inner life of God is available to men and women *through Jesus*. When John speaks of 'Truth' he does not mean mere sincerity of heart. He is talking about the *inner reality* of God's being, which has never been fully seen, but which now has become visible *through Jesus*.

When you realise that, it is easy to see that far from endorsing a kind of bland universalism in these words 'spirit and truth', Jesus is in fact doing the very opposite. He tells us here that it is no more a case of everybody worshipping God in his own way in the new Christian era than it was before. Truly, the exclusiveness of the Jews has been demolished. But it has been replaced by a new kind of particularism—the exclusiveness of Jesus. True worshippers must worship the Father in spirit and truth, and what John means by these words can relate only to who Jesus is and what he has done. 'I am the way and the truth and the life,' Jesus will assert a lttle later. 'No-one comes to the Father except through me' (14:6).

It is, then, only people who have received the spiritual life and the spiritual reality of God which Jesus brings who are those true worshippers for whom God is looking in this new day. It is a heart-response, all right; but not to some vague generalised idea of God. It is a heart-response to Jesus himself.

A commitment to Jesus

'I know that Messiah' (called Christ) 'is coming. When he comes, he will explain everything to us.' Then Jesus declared, 'I who speak to you am he' (4:25–26).

If you are going to get the full power of that final affirmation by Jesus, you have to realise that what John actually wrote was not 'I who am speaking to you am he,' but 'I who am speaking to you; *I am*.' To a person like this woman, familiar with the Old Testament, such a bald and unqualified use of the first person of the verb 'to be' would be shatteringly bold, perhaps even blasphemous. Long before, Moses had stood before God at the burning bush and asked God for his name. 'When I speak to the people, what shall I tell them you're called?'

'I am that I am,' replied God, 'tell them *I am* has sent you. That is my name.'

So Jesus here is not only claiming to be the Messiah. He is

as good as claiming identity with God: 'I am.' It is a majestic statement. It means that this eternal life he has been talking about, this water which will satisfy us, is not an article that we can add to our list of personal possessions. No; Jesus is the divine life personified. He gives us life by giving himself to us. The answer to our need is not a new religious technique, not even a new religious experience. It is a relationship with him, the Living One. It is to such a relationship that Jesus invites this woman at the close of their conversation. Just look at the effect it has on her.

> Leaving her water jar . . . (4:28)

John is a master of such apparently incidental detail. The symbol of her emptiness lies abandoned there at his feet. She had found the living water, for she had found Jesus! Things would never be the same again.

It can be the same for you.

The steps are simple: a stimulated curiosity, a conscious need, an awakened conscience, a heart response, and a personal commitment.

Perhaps as you read this you are aware of being somewhere along that chain of conversation with Jesus, too. If so, then stop pretending you are OK. Face up to the fact that you are empty. Stop trying to blame other things, and accept the fact that it is your moral failure that has broken the tie between you and God and left you in this vacuum of emptiness you feel. Commit yourself to Jesus. Jesus does not ask that you abandon your cultural identity. He does not give you a long list of rules to keep, or rituals to perform. He simply says, 'Come to me, realising who I am, and ask me for the water of life.'

3
The Son

John 5:16–47

Jesus has always been a controversial figure. There is nothing unusual about that, of course. Controversy has surrounded many great and important men of history. But the debate about Jesus is rather a special one. Normally it is a man's ideas that provoke the argument. Take for instance a thinker like Karl Marx. He is controversial because of the revolutionary political and economic theories that he espoused. Or take a man like Sigmund Freud; he was the source of enormous outrage in his day because of the bizarre and unconventional explanations he gave of mental illness. The quarrels which these seminal thinkers have generated in our century all centre around the opinions they had. And I think you will find that is the way it is with 99.9% of all controversies.

But with Jesus it's different. With few exceptions, the ideas of Jesus are universally applauded. Which of us would want to quarrel with his ethic? 'Love your neighbour as yourself' . . . 'Turn the other cheek' . . . 'Sell what you have and give to the poor'. Everyone agrees upon the wisdom and laudability of this kind of advice. The moral values of Jesus have rarely, if ever, been contradicted. On the contrary, they have been a source of inspiration to multitudes both of Christians and non-Christians alike.

No, unlike Marx and Freud, what makes Jesus controversial is not the ideas that he expressed but the person he

was. If Christians had been prepared to call Jesus just a
great man, or a philosopher, or genius, even a prophet,
there would have been no controversy about him at all. He
would have gone down in history as a saint and have been
revered by just about everybody. It was not what he *taught,*
but who he *was* that has caused the argument. Christianity
has been a controversial religion simply because Christians
have insisted that no category was sufficient to contain their
Master, except the category of divinity itself. Jesus was
God, they say; God in the flesh.

It is that which provokes the humanist's contempt,
which inspires the Muslim's rage, which severed Christianity from its Jewish roots and which is still today the major
obstacle to faith for many thinking people. 'I can accept the
Sermon on the Mount,' they say. 'It's the supernatural
dimensions with which you Christians invest your Jesus that
I find so difficult.' Well, in this chapter I want us to examine
that controversy about the person of Jesus. I want us to
think about why it is that Christians confess Jesus as God
and about the great issues that hang upon that confession.

The extraordinary claim (verses 16–23)

'My Father is always at his work to this very day, and I, too, am
working.' For this reason the Jews tried all the harder to kill
him; not only was he breaking the Sabbath, but he was even
calling God his own Father, making himself equal with God
(5:17–18).

According to John, the controversy about Jesus' divinity
had already begun during the years of his public ministry in
Palestine. That is really an enormously important observa-
tion, for this reason. For some time now, the most heated
debate about the person of Jesus has not been taking place
outside the church at all, but inside it. The ordinary Christian who has no pretensions to theological expertise
probably looks back to 1963 as the watershed in this regard. It

was in that year that John Robinson, then Bishop of Wool-wich, published a notorious book called *Honest to God*.

In it he argued, among other things, that the old credal formulae by which the church back in the fifth century had sought to express the divine nature of Jesus were meaning-less to the modern world. The whole idea of God coming to earth in the shape of a man was a fantastic fairy tale, he said; and it would have to be acknowledged as such. To be fair, Robinson was not by any means the first person to say such things, but that book did represent the first surfacing in the public eye of a theological revolution that had been going on in this century.

Since then the christological debate has continued to make news. In 1971, for example, the Reverend Michael Taylor, Principal of Northern Baptist College, similarly denied the deity of Jesus Christ in a public address. He prompted a huge correspondence in the *Baptist Times* and the affair eventually resulted in the secession of a number of Baptist churches from the Baptist Union. Then in 1977 it hit the headlines again, in an Anglican context this time, with a symposium called *The Myth of God Incarnate*. In the years since the publication of that book one of its authors, Don Cupitt, a Cambridge scholar, has repeatedly been at the forefront of the controversy. He has pushed it into the public eye both by his books and by his television series. His most recent offering, *The Sea of Faith,* was first screened on BBC Television on Sunday evenings in 1984. He not only questions whether Jesus is God, but whether there is such a thing as a God for Jesus to be.

The root of all this scholarly attack on the traditional Christian view of Jesus goes very deep and involves a whole host of complex issues to which we can't really do justice here. But there is a fundamental assumption which under-lies almost all of this scepticism, and without which it simply collapses. That is the assumption that there is a radical discontinuity between the original Jesus of history and the later Jesus of the church's confessional statements.

Scholars like Cupitt and Robinson insist that an alien 'God-incarnate' identity has been superimposed upon the Jesus of history by Christians who came after him. They insist that Jesus never claimed deity, nor did his immediate circle of acquaintances attribute deity to him. They say it was only when Christianity moved outside its Palestinian origins into the pagan world of Greek philosophy and religion that this divine nature was assigned him. Hence their favourite adjective is 'mythological'.

The deity of Jesus, they say, is a 'mythological' statement. That is not quite the same thing as saying it is false. According to them, it is a tool by which the early Christians sought to express the enormous significance Jesus had for them. But it is not rooted in objective facts. It is a pious fiction. Today, they say, we have outgrown such myths and need new conceptual tools by which to understand what Jesus should mean for us.

To use their word, we must 'de-mythologise' Jesus. This particular point of view is pressed with intimidating scholarly confidence in books by these theologians. It is often not so much argued as assumed that anybody who knows anything about it will accept the indisputability of this primary assumption; and Christians who wish to take a less sceptical, more conservative line are often treated with a patronising contempt.

I want to take issue with what I can only call this conspiracy of academic terrorism, by which many humble Christians are being quite needlessly shaken in their faith and many non-Christians quite irresponsibly confirmed in their unbelief. No one can deny that the church's understanding of Jesus' deity was developed and refined in the years after his death. No one can deny that the great Council of Chalcedon, which eventually formulated the doctrine of the divine and human nature of Jesus, used vocabulary which was indebted more to Greek philosophy than the Bible.

But I insist that our understanding of Jesus as God is
not a pious myth invented by second-century Christians.
It is rather a doctrine that evolved, like the flower from
the bud, as an inevitable consequence of the divine consciousness of Jesus himself; a consciousness which he
expressed verbally in the days of his flesh and which his
contemporaries clearly recognised albeit with a sense of
outrage. That is the eyewitness-testimony of John in this
chapter. It can be denied only by calling John a downright liar, and a hypocrite to boot, because nobody in the
New Testament speaks more about the importance of
truth than John does.

'He called God his own Father, making himself equal
with God.' There was nothing particularly unusual, of
course, about a Jew calling God 'Father'. The point John
is making here is that the Jews recognised that Jesus was
using this title in a particularly exclusive and personal
manner. He did not say 'Our Father' as they would have
done. He said 'My Father'. He did not speak of himself
as *a son* of God. He spoke of himself as *the Son*. The way
he talked clearly suggested to these Jews who were listening to him that he claimed a filial relationship to God
which was utterly unique to himself. He called God his
own Father, peculiarly so; and that is what offended
them. They were not so naive as to miss the implications
of that. Such a claim, they realised, made Jesus equal
with God.

The astonishing thing is that Jesus, according to John,
knowing that such an interpretation of his words and his
attitudes was being expressed, instead of repudiating it as a
blasphemous slander merely qualified and endorsed it.

> I tell you the truth, the Son can do nothing by himself; he can
> only do what he sees his Father doing, because whatever the
> Father does the Son also does (5:19).

In the five verses that follow we discover some of the

most extraordinary claims that any human being has ever made. First of all, Jesus says that his deeds are *divine deeds*. They are a perfect reproduction in miniature of the cosmic activity of God. 'He can only do what he sees his Father doing.' That's why he healed on the Sabbath contrary to Jewish law; because as God the Father did not stop making people better on Saturdays, no more could he. That was his rationale. But his imitation of the Father did not stop there. *Whatever* the Father does, the Son does too.

He is like one of those angled mirrors you sometimes see in a cathedral, by which they show you the gothic ceiling. Everything that God is, Jesus reflects horizontally out to the world around. As the apostle Paul would put it, he is the image of the invisible God.

What is more, Jesus goes on to claim that his knowledge is *divine knowledge*.

> The Father loves the Son and shows him all he does (5:20).

Prophets at best enjoyed a partial and hazy glimpse of God; but Jesus is claiming here that his contemplation of the Father was complete, unlimited, undistorted, born of a quite extraordinary intimacy. He totally embraced the mystery of God's being in his spiritual vision, far beyond anything any human being had ever experienced before.

Thirdly, Jesus claims *divine prerogative*. Life and death lie in his hands, he tells us.

> Just as the Father raises the dead and gives them life, even so the Son gives life to whom he is pleased to give it (5:21).

Indeed the full dimensions of this extraordinary assertion are spelt out even more clearly.

> As the Father has life in himself, so he has granted the Son to have life in himself (5:26).

Ordinary human beings rely upon God for every breath

they take. We are dependent creatures. Like light bulbs, we are only alive while we are connected to the mains. Should that source of life be switched off, our lights go out. But not Jesus's. 'I am the mains,' he says. 'I am the source of life. And I have at my discretion the power to give life.' That was something which every Jew knew that only God could claim.

Fourthly, Jesus claims here *divine authority*.

> Moreover, the Father judges no-one, but has entrusted all judgements to the Son (5:22).

One of the most extraordinary things about Jesus is the way we constantly find him saying to people that their sins are forgiven. C.S. Lewis indicates the outrageousness of this in his book, *Mere Christianity* (Collins).

> This is so preposterous as to be comic. We can all understand how a man forgives offences against himself. You tread on my toe and I forgive you . . . . but what should we make of a man, himself untrodden on, who announced that he forgave you for treading on other men's toes? Asinine fatuity is the kindest description we should give of his conduct. Yet this is what Jesus did.

Just as if, in fact, he had the power to declare men innocent or guilty at the bar of God's justice; and it is clear from the passage that that is precisely the authority he did claim to have. It would be he who called men to account on the last day, and judged the world.

Lastly and most remarkable of all, Jesus claims here *divine worship*:

> That all may honour the Son just as they honour the Father (5:23).

It is not hard to imagine how scandalous that would have

been to his Jewish listeners. Many of them regarded it as idolatrous merely to bow down before the Roman Emperor and call him Lord. Yet Jesus insists here that men venerate him as they venerate God, drawing no distinction between the two. Indeed to fail to do so, he says, is in itself an act of sacrilege and profanity.

> He who does not honour the Son does not honour the Father, who sent him (5:23).

Even more remarkable; men and women did worship Christ. We have it on the authority not just of the New Testament, but also of first-century pagan authors, that the early Christians worshipped Christ as God. What more compelling evidence of the primitiveness of the church's confession of Jesus' deity do we need?

So Christ claimed divine deeds, divine knowledge, divine prerogatives, divine authority and divine worship. It is not surprising that the Jews said he was making himself equal to God. If these things do not amount to a claim to deity, what does constitute such a claim? Yet perhaps the most remarkable thing of all about these verses is that there is not the faintest suspicion of megalomania within them.

Jesus accomplishes an extraordinary feat. He makes his stupendous assertions sound for all the world as if he is issuing a modest disclaimer. 'I can do nothing by myself, I can only do what the Father does.' He claims personal omnipotence and personal helplessness in the same breath.

> By myself I can do nothing; I judge only as I hear . . . I seek not to please myself but him who sent me (5:30).

Jesus then sees himself not as a rival to God's throne but as a humble recipient of God's grace. Here is no arrogant grasping at deity, no conceited revelling in deity. Here is deity wrapped in meekness and lowliness of heart. For all his claims and divine titles, here is a man, an unpretentious and unassuming man, utterly emptied of self-assertion and pride. A man content to be subordinate and obedient to God the Father. Here is Man as we are meant to be, Man in the image of God. In a word, here is incarnation: true God, perfect Man. Here is the paradox that we can never resolve, the equation we can never solve: one plus one equals one. Two wills but one purpose, two persons but one life.

It is no wonder that the early Christians had such a struggle to formulate their doctrine of the person of Jesus. One must have some sympathy for them. It is no wonder either that theologians today are dissatisfied with their work. But we can be sure of this. That early conviction that Jesus and God were one was no invention born of theological imagination. It was the product of witness they received from the mouth of Jesus himself—that is John's claim.

It will not do therefore to make out that Jesus was an ordinary human being to whom subsequent generations ascribed the status of divinity. On the contrary, according to those who knew him, Jesus himself made it impossible for them to come to any other conclusion by his own divine consciousness. Again C.S. Lewis in his book *Mere Christianity* (Collins) expresses it very well.

> People often say . . . . 'I'm ready to accept Jesus as a great moral teacher, but I don't accept His claim to be God.' That is the one thing we must not say. A man who is merely a man and said the sort of things Jesus said would not be a great moral teacher. He would either be a lunatic—on a level with the man who says he is a poached egg—or else he would be the Devil of Hell. You must make your choice. Either this man was, and is, the Son of God: or else a madman or something worse. You can shut Him up for a fool, you can spit at Him and kill Him as a demon; or you can fall at His feet and call Him Lord and God. But let us not come up with any patronising nonsense about His being a great human teacher. He has not left that open to us.

The rejected evidence (verses 30–47)

> You diligently study the Scriptures because you think that by
> them you possess eternal life. These are the Scriptures that tes-
> tify about me yet you refuse to come to me to have life (5:39).

If you have followed my argument so far, you are probably thinking: 'If Jesus made such claims as these, why is it
that so many liberal theologians of our day deny his deity
and insist it's a second-century Christian myth?'

The answer is quite simple. These theologians deny the
deity of Jesus for the same reason these Jews denied it—
because they do not accept the evidence. Jesus in this passage cites four types of evidence about his own person. The
Jews rejected them all. So do many liberal theologians of
today.

First of all, he cites the evidence of *his own claims*. He
freely accepts that on their own these would lack credibility:

> If I testify about myself my testimony is not valid (5:31).

Jesus is not suggesting that his own divine consciousness
can be ignored. But he is saying that if a man were to turn
up in a church and claim to be the Son of God, most people
would not immediately conclude that a miracle had happened. Most would conclude that somebody had just
escaped from a mental hospital. That would not be an
unreasonable assumption in the absence of any supporting
evidence. It was a rule of Jewish law that evidence had to be
corroborated if it was to be accepted. Jesus recognises the
wisdom of that. His claims are stupendous. It is unrealistic
to expect people merely to take his word for it. But he is
equally clear that confirmatory evidence was available to
those who were willing to heed it.

> There is another who testifies in my favour and I know that his testimony about me is valid (5:31).

It is pretty certain that this 'another' to whom Jesus is referring is the Father himself. After all, it's from the Father that Jesus gained his own confidence of his divine Sonship, and it is from a similar experience of the Father that he is telling us here that any who are going to believe in his Sonship must receive inner conviction on the point.

This is not to say that the divinity of Jesus is something that can be perceived only by some kind of mystical intuition. No, as Jesus goes on to say, there are concrete, objective evidences through which this divine testimony is further confirmed. First, there is the evidence of *believing men and women*, such as John the Baptist. People had been to John and *he had testified to the truth*. Once again Jesus is anxious to disabuse us of any thought that the testimony of Christian believers can prove who he is.

> Not that I accept human testimony; but I mention it that you may be saved (5:34).

When you think about it, no human being can prove the divine authority of Jesus, for the simple reason that there is no human authority sufficiently great from which such an accreditation might validly be drawn. Only God can authenticate God.

But, says Jesus, though human beings are fallible and cannot prove my divinity, there is a valid persuasive force in human testimony:

> John was a lamp that burned and gave light, and you chose for a time to enjoy his light (5:35).

In other words, if a man of undisputed integrity and spiritual sensitivity points to Jesus and says he is the One who has come from heaven, the Son to whom the Father gives the Spirit without limit, then that is surely significant. It may not prove anything in a technical sense, but it surely removes the divinity of Jesus from the realm of the utterly implausible.

Everybody was agreed, Jesus says to his listeners, that John the Baptist was somebody special. Important people were prepared to go along and be seen in public conversation with him and bathe a little in his reflected light. Why then were they so fickle as to discount the testimony he bore to Jesus?

One can say the same today on a much grander scale. Look at the history of the world and consider the many great men who have been utterly convinced of the divine identity of Jesus: men of great holiness, huge intellect, men of vast public reputation. Think of some of the people you know personally who are Christians. Do you really think such people are dupes, or hypocrites, or deceivers?

Just consider the church today. When scholars affirm so emphatically that modern man cannot possibly believe in a supernatural Jesus, I am tempted to ask in which particular ivory tower do they spend their waking moments? For it is not the churches that preach the anaemic and philosophical Jesus of liberal theology that are packed to the doors today. It is those that stand for the old orthodox Jesus. True God and true Man. Indeed if the evidence of television audiences figures is anything to go by, contemporary theologians have a long way to go to catch up on Billy Graham.

So are we so arrogant as to dismiss all these believing men and women as naive and gullible? The fact is that these sceptical theologians who claim to speak for the modern world do nothing of the sort. They speak for no one but their own pretentious little coterie of avant-garde philosophers. The masses of Christian people are still on the side of John the Baptist.

Then, Jesus cites the evidence of *his own life and works*.

I have testimony weightier than that of John. For the very work

that the Father has given me to finish, and which I am doing,
testifies that the Father has sent me (5:36).

There is a story I rather like about the nineteenth century
artist, Paul Doré. He was travelling in a foreign country and
lost his passport. He found himself confronted by a very
suspicious immigration official at a border. 'I'm sorry,' he
said, 'I've lost my identification documents. But I can tell
you I'm Paul Doré the painter.'

'Ah,' said the sceptical guard, 'well, we will soon see
about that.' So he gave him a pencil and paper. 'Prove it!'
he said. Whereupon Doré made a lightning sketch of some
nearby travellers with such inimitable skill that the official
could only say, 'There is no question about it—you must be
Doré!'

That may be a fanciful story, but it is true that unique
men carry their own credentials with them. Jesus did not
need a passport saying 'Country of origin—Heaven.
Father's name—God. Occupation—Saviour of the
World.' His very deeds were evidence in themselves, those
works which the Father had given him to do. Often when
John uses the word 'works', he speaks specifically of the
miracles Jesus did, so that in all probability that is the primary reference here. These Jews had just seen a chronic
invalid healed by Jesus at the pool of Bethesda. Such supernatural signs surrounded Jesus on a scale so prolific they
have never been equalled before or since. 'Don't you
realise,' he says, 'these are not just wonders to amaze you?
They are signs, God-given pointers to direct you to my
divine identity.'

The same evidence is available today. Even if we treat
the Gospel records only as uninspired human reminis-
cences of Jesus, it is impossible to avoid the conclusion that
Jesus was a supernatural person. In the last century
attempts were made by liberal scholars to sift the Gospel
material cutting out all the miraculous elements in Jesus'

story. They were sure that underneath all these accretions to Jesus, they would discover a coherent picture of a perfectly non-miraculous Jewish rabbi with a purely ethical message.

But it is now widely agreed that that attempt failed miserably. History does not witness to any other than a supernatural Jesus. The supernaturalness of Jesus is woven into the warp and woof of the historical testimony to him in a way which cannot be cut out. There is no such historical animal as a non-supernatural Jesus. As far as any historical research can discover Jesus was in his own day what Peter claimed just after Jesus' death. 'Jesus of Nazareth was a Man attested to you by God with mighty works and wonders and signs which God did through him in your midst as you yourselves know' (Acts 2:22).

But the Jews, just as they refused to believe the testimony of John the Baptist, refused also to believe the weightier testimony of Jesus' miracles. It is, of course, precisely the same with sceptical twentieth-century scholars. They are not prepared to accept a supernatural Jesus whatever the evidence for it in the gospels may be. They would rather believe that the gospels are a tissue of fantasy and fabrication than accept such a conclusion. If you ask, however, why are they so reluctant to accept a supernatural Jesus it has got nothing to do with the nature of the historical evidence. It has everything to do with their own philosophical presuppositions. Miracles are unbelievable in a modern world. They are 'unscientific'.

What nonsense! If science has made progress in our generation, it is precisely by taking seriously anomalous observations. The graph that was not quite straight. The number that was not quite right. The pattern that wasn't quite symmetrical. True science never dismisses anomalies on the grounds that they do not fit current theories. It reshapes its theories to accommodate them. And Jesus is challenging his doubters here to do the same thing with him. Of course the miracles he performed before many witnesses were anomalies. Otherwise they would not be miracles. The open-minded response, however, is not to say 'such things are impossible—they must be fiction,' but rather to say 'if such things happened they are extraordinary; and the Person concerned must be an extraordinary Person.'

There is nothing unscientific at all about taking seriously the possibility of the miraculous. What is unscientific is to act as the scholars of Padua did when they refused to look down Galileo's telescope for fear of seeing what they did not want to see. To shut your eyes to the possibility that Jesus could be God and refuse to give him the opportunity to prove otherwise—that is being unscientific.

Lastly, Jesus cites here the evidence of *the Bible*.

> The Father who sent me has himself testified concerning me
> . . . . You diligently study the Scriptures because you think by
> them you possess eternal life. These are the Scriptures that tes-
> tify about me (5:37, 39).

The scepticism of these Jews is so ironic, because nobody studied the Bible harder than they did. Yet Jesus says that in spite of all their study they totally missed the conclusion to which the Bible, in the intention of God, was designed to bring them. So, in a strangely similar way, have liberal theologians of the twentieth century. Many of them are outstandingly fine biblical scholars, and we should not underestimate that. But like these Jews their scholarship is spiritually sterile. It may lead to doctorates. It does not lead to life.

Notice the reasons that Jesus gives for the blindness of these Jews to the witness of his divinity in Scripture. First, he says that it was because of a fundamental lack of personal knowledge of God on their part.

> You have never heard his voice nor seen his form, nor does his
> word dwell in you, for you do not believe the one he sent
> (5:37–38).

Every now and then I have to give references for people applying for jobs or colleges, and there is one question which is always at the top of the form. *How long have you known the applicant?* They ask this because they know better than to put weight upon the opinion of somebody who has no personal acquaintance with their candidate.

Yet so often, I fear, those who destroy the credibility of Jesus in the minds of ordinary men and women are themselves totally without any personal experience of God. All too often, if the truth were known, they are worldly-minded, career academics. Like these Jews, they study Moses in their libraries but they have never stood before a burning bush in their lives. That is one reason why they cannot see the divinity of Jesus in the Scriptures which they study—they lack a personal knowledge of God who wrote them.

The second reason Jesus hints at here is because they study the Bible the wrong way.

You *diligently* study the Scriptures.

The word he uses has the flavour of minute analysis or microscopic scrupulousness. In the case of these Jews, of course, this scrutiny was in the interest of scribal accuracy. So devoted to the Bible were they, they demonstrated an almost superstitious reverence for every letter and punctuation mark in the sacred text. Today scholarly investigation is every bit as meticulous, but it is usually in the interest of textual criticism rather than of textual reproduction.

Nevertheless Jesus' point is equally valid. For in both cases it is a scholarship which for all its intensity never goes beyond the academic. It isn't really motivated by an urgent sense of personal need. At best it is motivated by intellectual fascination, at worst by professional ambition.

Which brings us to the third reason Jesus says they were

blind to his divinity. They were more concerned about their scholarly reputation than they were about God's truth.

> I have come in my Father's name, and you do not accept me; but if someone else comes in his own name, you will accept him. How can you believe if you accept praise from one another, yet make no effort to obtain the praise that comes from the only God? (5:43–44).

What a subtle trap this is, and how many great scholars have fallen into it. The prevailing tide of scholarly opinion says that Jesus is a charlatan. Many notable rabbis have written papers in the *Jerusalem Journal of Theology* to prove the point. Only a lecturer who wants to look like a fool in the senior common room would dare to say anything to the contrary. So scholarship conspires to conceal the truth by its own mutual admiration society.

But fourthly and perhaps most important of all, the reason that they were blind is that they had misunderstood the purpose of Scripture.

> You diligently study the Scriptures because you think that by them you possess eternal life (5:39).

What are you saying, Jesus? Are you suggesting they were wrong in that? Surely eternal life *is* to be found in the Bible? The strict answer to that is yes, and no. According to Jesus eternal life is there in the Scripture but it is there only because *he* is there.

> These are the Scriptures that testify about me yet you will not come to me to have life (5:39–40).

The Bible is God's testimony to his Son. Its purpose is to direct men on divine authority to Jesus as the source of life. The Bible is a signpost. It cannot give life itself. It can only point you to the One in whom life can be found. It's a prescription. It cannot cure sin, but it can specify the medicine that will. It is vital that those of us who call ourselves evangelical understand this. The Bible is never an end in itself. And if we are ever found treating it as such, we fall into the trap of which some validly accuse us; bibliolatry, worshipping a divine book rather than its divine author.

Of course we value the Bible highly, but we do so because it is the Father's testimony to Jesus. We treasure it in the same way that a girl treasures her lover's letter, because it speaks to us of him. Bible study can never be an end in itself. It is a pilgrimage intended to lead us to an ever deeper and more intimate knowledge of Christ. We must remember that. But if evangelical Christians need to understand this purpose of Scripture, the liberal Christian needs to understand it even more. For the fallacy of the liberal scholar is that he can find eternal life without the Scriptures. He can tear down the signpost and still find the pathway. He can mutilate the prescription and still take the medicine. So as far as he is concerned, the Scriptures are not an authoritative divine testimony to anything, least of all to the divinity of Jesus Christ. To the scholar they are just a jumble of garbled folk tales, pious myths with just the occasional snippet of real history thrown in.

Consequently, they come to the Scriptures in essentially the same way as the Jews did, in order to confirm their own sceptical preconceived ideas about Jesus. They have no intention of discovering a divine Jesus in these pages. When they open its pages, their minds are already closed to the possibility of such a result.

You refuse to come to me to have life (5:40).

Like Nelson, who put the telescope to his blind eye, they

see no God made flesh, because they choose not to see him.
But we can be sure of this, the root of their blindness lies
not in their intellects, great though they may be, but in their
wills: 'You *refuse* to come to me.' That, of course, is the
final irony.

> Do not think I will accuse you before the Father. Your accuser
> is Moses, on whom your hopes are set. If you believed Moses,
> you would believe me, for he wrote about me. But since you do
> not believe what he wrote, how are you going to believe what I
> say? (5:45–47).

This is the tragic end, says Jesus, of all such sceptical
Bible scholars. On the last day it will not be Jesus who con-
demns them. The very authors of the biblical books they
have pored over with such sterile diligence will rise to indict
them of their unbelief. For those who cannot believe in the
Scripture cannot believe in Christ, for the only Christ there
is, is the Christ of Scripture.

The critical decision (verses 24–29)

> I tell you the truth, whoever hears my word and believes him
> who sent me has eternal life and will not be condemned; he has
> crossed over from death to life (5:24).

There is a fascinating nuance in John's use of words
here, because he does not actually say *from* death to
life. To be strictly accurate he says *out of* death into life.
In other words, he thinks of death and life not so much
as descriptions of a man's physical condition but as
spiritual spheres or environments within which a man
exists. It is almost as though John imagines death and
life as parallel universes. One is converging to extinc-
tion, and the other expanding into an ever-richer possibility of experience.

By nature, he says, we all start in the shrinking world of

death. If our situation were not to change, we would be doomed to perish along with that dying universe. But something has changed. Jesus has come. It is because Jesus is the unique person that he is that we have hope. For Jesus is a singularity in space and time, a man from that other world, precipitated into our dying one. He is a man who has life in himself, yet has broken into the sphere of death. He has thus created in his own person an interface between the two, a corridor leading from the world of death to that of life. 'I am the door. I am the way. I am the life.' It is the unique person he is that makes that access possible.

Furthermore men and women are already passing through that spiritual passageway which is Jesus.

> I tell you the truth, a time is coming and has now come when the dead will hear the voice of the Son of God and those who hear will live (5:25).

So eternal life is not something for which a Christian waits. It is a sphere of existence into which he has already passed through Jesus. One day that new identity he has in the other universe is going to become a glaringly obvious reality to everybody.

> Do not be amazed at this, for a time is coming when all who are in their graves will hear his voice and come out—those who have done good will rise to live, and those who have done evil will rise to be condemned (5:28–29).

The controversy which we have discussed in this chapter is not a mere academic debate. It is a life and death issue! In the first chapter of Don Cupitt's *Sea of Faith,* Cupitt tells how, as a young curate, he was called to a deathbed at Salford Royal Hospital. It was three in the morning. The patient was alone and unconscious and within a few minutes he was dead. Cupitt says that he gave the rite of absolution but afterwards wondered what had he really done. 'I did not hold the magical view that giving him the last rites would actually alter his eternal destiny from what it would otherwise have been,' he says. 'And yet I still thought it had been worthwhile. I hope somebody else does the same for me when my time comes' (*Sea of Faith*, BBC Publications). Religion, according to him, is a way of affirming human dignity in the face of an indifferent universe.

Don't you find that sad? I find it pathetic. Here is a scholar of Cambridge University. A theologian of the first order and that is the best he can offer: symbols without substance, sacraments without significance, religion without rationality. Is that anaemic nonsense the faith that will steer us into the next millennium? People at the end of the twentieth century need hope not platitudes. They need salvation not sentimentality.

Jesus is not offering us here an affirmation of human dignity in the face of an indifferent universe. He offers us personal access through his divine person into a new universe. Supernatural? Of course it's supernatural.

Jesus is a supernatural person. He claims to be so. Men and women of God throughout the ages confess him to be so. His mighty deeds confirm him to be so. The Bible declares him to be so. When I have got only three more minutes to live, I will need no yawning, sceptical priest to come to my bed-side to affirm my human dignity with empty cant, because I will have the Son of God himself at my right hand. He will be saying to me 'I am the resurrection and the life. He who believes in me will live, even though he dies' (11:25).

Tell me, when you have got only three minutes to live, who would you rather be: sceptic or believer? Jesus puts us on the spot here. He calls us to make a decision. We may join the ranks of the sceptics and refuse to come to him so that we may have life. Or we may place our faith in him and

join the ranks of those believers who are proving the truth
of his promise.

> Whoever hears my word and believes him who sent me has
> eternal life and will not be condemned; he has crossed over
> from death to life (5:24).

4

The Bread

John 6:25–65

'Let's consider your age to begin with—how old are you?'

'I'm seven and a half exactly.'

'You needn't say "exactly",' the Queen remarked: 'I can believe it without that. Now I'll give *you* something to believe. I'm just one hundred and one, five months and a day.'

'I can't believe *that*!' said Alice.

'Can't you?' the Queen said in a pitying tone. 'Try again: draw a long breath, and shut your eyes.'

Alice laughed. 'There's no use trying,' she said: 'one *can't* believe impossible things.'

'I daresay you haven't had much practice,' said the Queen. 'When I was your age, I always did it for half an hour a day. Why, sometimes I've believed as many as six impossible things before breakfast.' (Lewis Carroll, *Through the Looking Glass*.)

Lewis Carroll is, of course, commenting in his deceptively childish style on the enigma of faith. Why is it that some people manage to believe things which other people find utterly incredible? In the upside-down world of the White Queen it seems that faith was all a matter of effort. 'Hold your breath and shut your eyes,' she advises. 'You can believe anything if only you try hard enough.' But on this side of the looking glass we, like Alice, know that it is not that simple. There is all the difference in the world between faith and mere wishful thinking. To fail to observe

that distinction is to confuse reality with fantasy. Holding
your breath and shutting your eyes is not belief. It is make-
believe. And by definition, anything you have to make
yourself believe cannot be real, for reality constrains belief
effortlessly. As Alice puts it, 'It is no use trying,' because
'one just cannot believe impossible things.' Yet people do
so, and that is the mystery.

Take Christians, for instance. When you think about it in
the cold dispassionate light of reason, what Christians
believe is really quite extraordinary. God became Man and
walked about the earth! Alice could be excused for calling
it impossible. Yet Christians do not feel that they are forc-
ing themselves to believe the impossible. They are not playing a game of 'Let's pretend'. There is no self-hypnosis
involved. They believe under the constraint of what they
intuitively feel to be the truth.

How do Christians do that? It cannot just be a matter of
gullibility. No doubt there are Christians who are naive and
credulous, but it simply will not do to portray them all as
dimwits or dupes. There is an enigma here—the enigma of
faith. Some people have got it and others have not. The
question is why? Why do unbelievers not believe? How is it
believers find they can? That is the question I want us to
consider here as we study our fourth conversation with
Jesus.

The reasons unbelievers do not believe

(1) The spirituality of Jesus' message

> I tell you the truth, you are looking for me, not because you
> saw miraculous signs but because you ate the loaves and had
> your fill. Do not work for food that spoils, but for food that
> endures to eternal life, which the Son of Man will give you
> (6:26–27).

In order to understand what Jesus is saying here it is

necessary to look back over preceding events. Jesus has just
performed a most notable miracle by the side of the Sea of
Galilee, feeding a crowd of 5,000 people from the meagre
rations provided by a small boy's lunchbox. Inevitably it
caused a stir; but not, apparently, the kind for which Jesus
was looking.

> After the people saw the miraculous sign that Jesus did, they
> began to say; 'Surely this is the Prophet who is to come into the
> world.' Jesus, knowing that they intended to come and make
> him king by force, withdrew again into the hills by himself
> (6:14–15).

It is important to remember that this is Galilee, where
feelings of antipathy towards the central Roman government ran very high. It was a place notorious for violent protests against the Romans, and where men were always on
the lookout for some new charismatic figure to lead them in
their efforts in this direction. Indeed their religion encouraged them to do so, for it laid great emphasis on the great
messianic prophecies of the Old Testament. Passages like
Deuteronomy 18 which they quote here in verse 14, where
God promises to send a prophet like Moses to the people.
Moses, the Galileans reasoned, had been a freedom fighter
liberating their forefathers from bondage to Pharaoh.
Surely, they thought, the Messiah when he came would be
a freedom fighter too, liberating them from their bondage
to Caesar.

Not only was this place Galilee; John also tells us in verse
4 that it was Passover time. Now Passover was to loyal Jews
in the first century what the Battle of the Boyne is to loyal
Protestants in Northern Ireland today. It was the historical
focus of all their political dreams. Every year they commemorated how God had triumphed over the forces of
Egypt and led their people out of the land of bondage,
across the Red Sea and into freedom. Passover was a time
of intense nationalist fervour. So if you wanted to start a

revolution in Judea, the best place to go was Galilee; and the best time to go there was Passover time.

So it is not surprising that these Galileans so quickly entertained revolutionary and political thoughts of Jesus. 'Let us make him King,' they said. His miracles had kindled hopes in them that their messianic expectations were at last being fulfilled. 'Perhaps this is the Prophet like Moses,' they wondered. 'This is the Passover we've been waiting for.' Yet what I want you to notice is that even while they were talking to one another in those tones, Jesus was escaping into solitude. He knew that they intended to come and make him king by force so he withdrew again into the hills by himself. And it is against the background of that reluctance on Jesus' part to accept the political role into which this crowd wanted to force him that we must understand these rather cryptic words, which he spoke to the same crowd after they had pursued him round the lake to Capernaum.

Do not work for food that spoils, but for food that endures to eternal life (6:27).

'What you Galileans have got to realise,' Jesus is saying, 'is that there are two kinds of bread. There is bread that nourishes our physical existence which is doomed one day to perish, but there is also bread that nourishes our spiritual existence which is destined to last for ever. And the trouble with you Galileans is that your whole mindset is orientated around the former. In a word, you are materialists. You ate the loaves and had your fill. You perceived the economic benefits of what happened on the other side of the Lake and you've got all excited about it. But you completely missed the spiritual significance of what happened!

'You may have seen a miracle but you did not see the sign. Don't you realise,' Jesus implies, 'that when I looked at that crowd by the Sea of Galilee I didn't just see a bundle of hungry bodies incapable of providing for themselves materially? I saw a multitude of human beings, searching in vain for something to satisfy that spiritual vacuum that was gnawing at their hearts. I didn't just see empty stomachs. I saw empty souls! And my willingness to feed them physically was just a symbol, a pointer, a sign of my willingness to meet that much deeper spiritual need.'

Jesus must offer the same advice to us in the twentieth century. We must not misunderstand him. Jesus never said that issues of political freedom or economic justice were unimportant. No one could accuse Jesus of being indifferent to the plight of the poor and the oppressed. But, uncongenial as it was to the political activists of Jesus' own day and uncongenial as it is to the political activists of the present, the fact remains, Jesus was not a political messiah. He could have been, but he chose not to be. He faced a world in its own way just as militarily insecure, just as socially divided, just as economically deprived as our own. But he faced it with a message that was unashamedly spiritual in its emphasis.

It is vital we understand that. For throughout history there has been a tendency within the church to politicise the Christian message. One can sympathise with the phenomenon. We are, rightly, passionate in our concern for justice and freedom. When we feel that way it is all too easy to identify the kingdom of God with the progressive and the radical political ethos of our day. But it simply will not do! For Jesus was *not* a political messiah. There were plenty of zealot revolutionaries around in Galilee in those days. He had every opportunity to be one had he wanted to be, but he did not. He categorically refused to endorse the politicised aspirations of this Galilean mob, in the same way that he earlier refused to accept Satan's offer of power as the route to his kingdom. It is true that he spoke of a kingdom. But he would not let them make him king, for the very simple reason that the kingdom of God about which he spoke and the kingdom of God they had in mind were completely different.

Indeed, if you read John's gospel carefully, one of the things that you will discover is that John, unlike the synoptic evangelists, goes out of his way to avoid the phrase 'kingdom of God' altogether. He probably did so in order to evade exactly the kind of politicised misunderstanding of that phrase in which these Galileans would have so happily indulged. John chooses to speak not of the 'kingdom of God' but of 'eternal life'. As far as he is concerned, those two ideas are synonymous. For Jesus' message is a spiritual one, a message not about food for the body, but about food for the soul.

At the end of this chapter we discover that it was precisely because of the spirituality of Jesus' message that, in the end, the Galilean peasantry abandoned him. The same thing happens today. If we could stand up and offer Christ as the One who can tell us how to implement our utopian dreams of distributive justice and international disarmament, then thousands would flock to Jesus. It is because he tells us to be less concerned about our physical bodies and more concerned about our eternal souls that he is treated with contempt by those who are looking for political answers to Man's problems.

(2) The supernaturalism of Jesus' claims

> At this the Jews began to grumble about him because he said, 'I am the bread that came down from heaven.' They said, 'Is this not Jesus, the son of Joseph, whose father and mother we know? How can he now say, "I came down from heaven"?' (6:41–42).

If you look again at the last chapter you will recall the extraordinary statements that Jesus made concerning himself in John 5. There, of course, he was in conversation with the conservative and scholarly rabbis of the city of

Jerusalem. In this chapter he is in controversy with quite a different audience, the militant peasants of rural Galilee. And yet there is something that you will observe which these two discourses have in common; and that is the egocentricity of Jesus' words—an egocentricity which, as we said earlier, one could only call megalomaniac if it were not coupled with the most extraordinary modesty.

Seventeen times in verse 34–40 Jesus uses the words 'I' or 'me' or 'my'. Most of us would consider it bad manners to talk so much about ourselves. But Jesus does not seem in the least embarrassed about it. Just look at the assertions which he makes in the midst of all those first person pronouns.

> I have come down from heaven not to do my own will but to do the will of him who sent me., And this is the will of him who sent me, that I shall lose none of all that he has given me, but raise them up at the last day (6:38–39).

He claims then *a divine origin*. 'I came down from heaven'. If somebody told us they had arrived in a flying saucer it would scarcely be less preposterous. He claims *a divine mission*. 'I am here to do the will of God who sent me.' And what is that will? Is it something nice and ordinary like being a doctor or a vicar? 'No,' says Jesus. 'My mission is to raise the dead'. King Canute was hardly less ambitious!

But most remarkable of all, and most central in this paragraph, he claims *a divine ministry*.

> I am the bread of life. He who comes to me will never go hungry, and he who believes in me will never be thirsty (6:35).

According to Jesus, the reason spiritual things must take precedence over material in our scale of priorities is because, in the final analysis, material things cannot really satisfy the human soul.

Human beings, Jesus reminds us, do not live by bread

alone. Life is more than meat. Of course for many people these days, such talk is a form of conservative seduction. As Marx said, religion is an opium to keep the poor content with their lot. But, according to Jesus, the truth is the very opposite. It is materialism that is the narcotic, which so anaesthetises people to the reality of spiritual things that real contentment, real satisfaction is rendered permanently inaccessible to them. All that the pursuit of material things does is to create in people an ascending spiral of acquisitive expectation that can never be appeased, in the same way that these Galileans could never be satisfied with one meal.

This year it is the new car, next year it will be the new washing machine and then the new video and after that the new house. It is insatiable. It never ends, because man is victim to spiritual hunger and no amount of material bread will appease it. Jean Paul Sartre, the novelist, was an atheist. But he once wrote of this human dilemma with painful honesty: 'That God does not exist I cannot deny, but that my whole being cries out for God I cannot forget.' That cry of the human spirit for something eternal around which to integrate itself is universal. We all feel it. You would not be reading this book if you did not feel it too. It is a fundamental need of the human soul.

A preacher in the Old Testament says that God has 'put eternity into our hearts'. But the extraordinary thing is that Jesus did not claim to feel that longing for spiritual satisfaction. He claimed to meet it. '*I* am the bread of life. He who comes to *me* will never go hungry. He who believes in *me* will never be thirsty.' That is remarkable! If you were to go to any clergyman and say that you have got a spiritual longing then if the clergyman was any good at all, he would direct you to God. He would say that God is the answer to that hunger and thirst in your soul. You must find him, and thus the solution of your problem. But Jesus did not say that. 'Come to *me*,' he said.

'If only you knew it,' he tells these Galilean militants, 'that supernatural manna you are looking for is staring you in the face. It is not a something but a Someone. It's me! I am not just the giver, I am the gift.'

> The bread of God is he who comes down from heaven and gives life to the world. I *am* the bread of life (6:33, 35).

But this was bread they just could not swallow. After all, Jesus was a local lad. If he had had angel's wings and arrived in a fiery chariot, it might have been different. But he was so ordinary, so human. 'Is this not Jesus the son of Joseph, whose father and mother we know? How can he now say "I came down from heaven"?' It seems ridiculous. It is one thing to go around working miracles. Quite another to go around claiming to be a miracle. But that was Jesus' assertion.

It remains his assertion today, and it is still an obstacle in the path of faith for many, many people. If Jesus had come and said to us that eternal life is a matter of giving to charity, there would be plenty of people willing to go out and buy their spiritual fire insurance with philanthropy. If Jesus had said that eternal life is a matter of practising yoga in your bedroom three times a day, there are thousands of people in this country who would gladly undertake that discipline. But Jesus said that eternal life was something we find by finding him. It is tied up with the supernatural person he is in himself. It is not a possession, but a relationship with him, the living One. And the response of many to that extraordinary supernaturalist claim is, 'Isn't this just Jesus, the son of Joseph? How can he say "I came down from heaven"?'

(3) The scandal of Jesus' cross

I am the living bread that came down from heaven. If a man

eats of this bread, he will live for ever. This bread is my flesh, which I will give for the life of the world. Then the Jews began to argue sharply among themselves, 'How can this Man give us his flesh to eat?' (6:51–52).

Jesus here engages in a very gruesome metaphor. Later Christian readers would undoubtedly have perceived some allusion to Holy Communion in the idea of eating Christ's flesh and blood. But Jesus could hardly have expected either his disciples or the crowd to understand his words in that way at this early point in time. No, Jesus is indicating here that the life of which he has been speaking will be mediated to the world through his violent death on the cross. The clue to understanding his language is to compare verse 54 with verse 40.

Whoever eats my flesh and drinks my blood has eternal life, and I will raise him up at the last day (6:54).

Everyone who looks to the Son and believes in him shall have eternal life, and I will raise him up at the last day (6:40).

The verses are closely parallel, the only difference being that one speaks of eating and drinking Christ's flesh and blood and the other of looking to him and believing in him. Jesus then is using parabolic language. He speaks not of a literal consuming of his flesh, but of a spiritual participation in his life. The brutal rending of his body in death would release the eternal life within him and make it available to all those who believe in him.

I tell you the truth, unless you eat the flesh of the Son of Man and drink his blood you have no life in you (6:53).

Just as the living Father sent me and I live because of the Father, so the one who feeds on me will live because of me (6:57).

I am the living bread that came down from heaven. If a man

eats this bread he will live forever. This bread is my flesh, which I will give for the life of the world (6:51).

If such words generate sacramental overtones in our minds it is because Holy Communion is also symbolical. It represents in a dramatic way precisely the same truth which Jesus is representing here in a metaphorical way. And familiarity with Holy Communion therefore helps us to accept and accommodate Jesus' words. But we must have some sympathy for the perplexity of his original hearers as they wrestle with this bizarre, cannibalistic figure of speech.

How can this man give us his flesh to eat? (6:52)

This is a hard teaching. Who can accept it? (6:60)

But notoice how Jesus responds.

Aware that his disciples were grumbling about this, Jesus said to them, 'Does this offend you? What if you see the Son of Man ascend to where he was before!' (6:61).

In other words, Jesus says, 'If you find my symbolic language gruesome or incomprehensible, how on earth are you going to cope with the real thing?' If Jesus had spoken in plainer terms about his cross, these Jews would have been even more offended. For the cross is a scandal to men and women, even when it's only spoken about indirectly as Jesus speaks about it here. That was Paul's experience at Corinth: 'We preach Christ crucified,' he wrote. 'To the Jews it is a stumbling block, to the Greeks it is foolishness.'

It is always so. The very idea of God having to suffer and die in public humiliation is to the unbelieving mind at best a ridiculous absurdity, at worst a blasphemous obscenity. However, it was not Paul who chose so unpopular a theme for his sermons but Christ himself who ordained that it must be so. 'For this bread is my flesh,' he says, which 'I will give for the life of the world.'

There were three causes of offence, then, three reasons for the unbeliever's unbelief: the spirituality of the message, the supernaturalism of Jesus' claims, and the scandal of the cross.

In fact, with so many intellectual obstacles in the way you may be thinking to yourself that faith is even more of an enigma than ever. It is a message so uncongenial to the materialist, so incredible to the rationalist, so offensive to just about anybody, that surely Jesus must have been tormented by the anxiety that no one would ever believe in him at all. But that is not the case, which brings us to the second element in our study:

The reason believers do believe

Three passages in this chapter tell us why there will always be believers.

> All that the Father gives me will come to me, and whoever comes to me I will never drive away (6:37).

> No-one can come to me unless the Father who sent me draws him, and I will raise him up at the last day (6:44).

> 'There are some of you who do not believe.' For Jesus had known from the beginning which of them did not believe and who would betray him. He went on to say, 'This is why I told you that no one can come to me unless the Father had enabled him' (6:64–65).

These three passages confront us with an area of biblical truth which many profess to find even more difficult and offensive than those of which we have been talking so far. Theologians in the past have sometimes called it the doctrine of effectual calling. Others, rather less happily, have referred to it as the doctrine of irresistible grace. It is a subject that has occasioned enormous debate.

Perhaps the easiest way of summarising it is to give you an illustration I once heard from Dr Jim Packer. When he was a student at Oxford, he had been punting on the river and fallen head first into the water. He said it was a most unpleasant experience because there were a lot of thick weeds that entangled his legs and his arms and the water was very deep. Indeed, he was afraid that he was going to drown because he just could not get to the shore. 'Imagine the possible reaction of some of my undergraduate colleagues in the boat,' he said. 'Some of them might have said, "Oh, you'll be all right, Jim, you can get out if only you try. Keep struggling!" Others might have said, "Oh, I'd like to help, old chap; but you see, I have a problem of conscience about interfering with people's free will. I can give you some tips on swimming, if you like."'

Dr Packer said that these two possible responses represent ways in which people have seen Christ's work of salvation throughout history. The first is called Pelagianism. Man has the natural ability to save himself if only he would work at it. It is the White Queen, telling Alice that she could believe if only she practised more. The second is called Arminianism. 'I'll assist you as much as I can, but there are limits to how much even God can help a human being.' It is the White Queen once more, offering advice on how to hold your breath and shut your eyes. But both of those ways of looking at the matter are saying, in one way or another, that if you want to be saved you must try harder; it is up to you; it is your self-effort that will get you there.

The question is: What do you do when you are, like Dr Packer, drowning because self-effort is not enough? When you feel like Alice that it is no use trying because 'I just can't believe impossible things?' What do you do in that situation? Packer pursued his illustration further and said how glad he was that on that particular occasion, when he fell into the river, his colleague in the boat behaved not as a

Pelagian or an Arminian, but as a Calvinist. He jumped personally into the water and overcame his friend's helpless struggles. He got him free of the weeds, brought him to the shore, gave him artificial respiration and put him back on his feet. As Dr Packer said, 'That's what I call a rescue!'

According to John 6, that is what Jesus calls a rescue too. He is fully aware of the insuperable obstacles that prevent sinful men and women from believing in him, the bread of life. He could see it in their eyes. But he was not discouraged because he knew that salvation was not ultimately a matter of self-effort, but of divine grace.

> No one can come to me unless the Father who sent me draws him (6:44).

It is God then that grants faith to men and women. He draws them to himself not with the crude tyranny of the rapist, but by the gentle wooing magnetism of a lover. By illuminating their minds, by renewing their affections, and by liberating their wills, he enables them to embrace him by faith. It is not a case of making themselves believe, but spontaneous, intuitive, effortless, through God's grace. And because Jesus knew that was the way it was, he could say, 'All the Father gives me will come to me.' There was no question in his mind about it. He could even say, 'I shall lose none of all that he has given me, but raise them up on the last day.' He did not ascend to heaven after his work on the cross was done wringing his hands in anxiety because no one might believe in him. No; he knew with calm certainty that God would draw people to him.

Some people profess to find this an offensive and a difficult element of the Bible's teaching. I have to tell you that I have never understood it that way. It is for me the only answer to the enigma of faith. I do not see how anybody believes anything as preposterous as the New Testament gospel unless it be by a miracle of divine grace.

It brings me encouragement as a preacher. It is disappointing when we preach our hearts out and find people going out through church doors unchanged. It is a comfort to realise that people walked away from Jesus' preaching just like that too. He was not demoralised by it: 'All that the Father gives me will come,' he said.

It is an encouragement to the believer too, because all of us at times in our lives have periods when our assurance is weak. 'How can I know I'm really going to heaven?' we say. 'How can I feel sure that I'm not going to fall away and perish?' The answer, of course, is that if salvation were a matter of our own efforts we never could be sure. But Jesus can give us security. 'I *will* raise them up on the last day,' he says. It is his hold on us, not ours on him, that counts in the long run.

But most of all, I believe that there is immense encouragement in this to the seeker. When Jesus says here, 'All that the Father gives me will come to me and whoever comes to me I will never drive away,' he means that it is not a case of our tormenting ourselves with futile questions as to whether we are on God's list or not. Such enquiries, says Jesus, are utterly pointless. The question he puts to us is 'Do we *want* to come to him?' Do we find in our hearts some glimmering of spiritual desire no matter how weak? Some concern for eternal things no matter how faint? Some attraction towards Jesus? Some faint stirring of faith in him? Do we feel anything of that?

If so, then praise God! For it is perfectly possible to translate verse 37 like this, 'Whoever is in process of coming to me I will never drive away.' If God were not drawing you, if he were not enabling you, if he were not giving you to Jesus, do you think for one moment that you would entertain such preposterous notions as Christians are supposed to believe? Do you suppose you would even give it serious consideration? Do you think you would give it even half-an-hour of your time?

See what Jesus says in verse 45. 'Everyone who listens to the Father and learns from him comes to me.' That is the way it is. Ask any Christian and you will discover that is how faith arrived for them. It was not an achievement that they congratulate themselves about. It was a *gift*. It was not the result of trying, but of listening, listening for the voice of God addressing them, informing them, calling them graciously to himself. That is the way it is. Of course there are plenty of things about Jesus that are hard to accept: the spirituality of his message, the supernaturalism of his person, the scandal of his cross. Every Christian has wrestled with those things. But, mercifully, faith is not a mere subscription to a creed, but a loving attachment to him, to Jesus. The question is not 'Do we understand everything he says?', but, 'Are we ready to commit ourselves to everything he is?'

Verse 66 says that from this time many of his disciples turned back and no longer followed him. You can just imagine what they were saying. 'Oh, we really thought after that miracle of the feeding of the 5,000 that he intended to bring about social reform, you know. But it seems he is just one of those religious cranks after all. Talking about pie-in-the-sky-when-you-die, a lot of super-spiritual claptrap about coming down from heaven and offensive gibberish about eating his flesh. It's a pity. A person with his gifts could have changed the world.'

'You do not want to leave too, do you?' Jesus asked the Twelve. Simon Peter answered him, 'Lord, to whom shall we go? You have the words of eternal life. We believe and know that you are the Holy One of God' (6:67–68).

5

The Light

John 8:12–36

By and large, people these days disapprove of controversy.
It frustrates us to see the endless debate in which rival fac-
tions indulge. In fact, it is more than frustrating; we find it
frightening too. For quarrelling so quickly leads to violence. That is why there is no doubt that most people today
take the view that we would be a lot better off without controversy. People should be less obstinate, they say; less
contradictory, more willing to compromise and make con-
cessions to one another. What a happy and peaceful world
it would be if only everybody would agree with one
another, wouldn't it? But unfortunately they never will.
That is one reason why Christianity is sometimes an
unpopular religion today. For, as everybody knows, Christians love a good argument. They have been arguing for
two thousand years. They argue both among themselves,
and with everybody else. Christianity has probably been
responsible for more controversy in this world than any
other single religion or philosophy in the history of man.
And it has not always stopped at hostile words. Christianity
has sometimes caused revolutions and wars. Some would
argue that in Northern Ireland it is still doing so.

That, of course, is why many people today claim that the
old style of Christianity will not do any more. It is too
aggressive, too intolerant, and too exclusive. If it is going to

further the cause of international peace and harmony, which is so important to us in the twentieth century, Christianity has got to change. There must be less dogmatism, they say, and more open-mindedness to other people's ideas.

You can see this trend all over the place—in the ecumenical movement for instance. 'It is time that Christian denominations forgot old animosities and closed ranks in one universal expression of ecclesiastical solidarity.' You see it too in the universalism of many of our contemporary theologians. Scholars such as Karl Rahner, for instance, suggest that we should stop distinguishing between Christians and non-Christians. We are all Christians really, he claims. Some of us know we are, while others of us do not. Or a scholar like John Macquarrie, who says that there is no longer any place for competitive proselytisation, and that what we need is a common mission, undertaken by all the great world religions in collaboration.

Indeed it is this trend towards tolerance that has made Eastern religions so attractive to some influential twentieth century Christian thinkers. New Age writers have emphasised that oriental mysticism is much more accommodating to the insights of other religions than Christianity has ever been. Why cannot we follow the lead of Annie Besant and the Theosophists, or Swami Vivekananda and the Vedantist movement, and look for a drawing together of the great faiths of the world in a global religious community?

It is a very appealing thought. I know not a few today who would argue that it is precisely what Jesus himself would have wanted; he talked so much about love, surely he could not have approved of all the aggression in which his followers have been engaged down through the centuries? He said, 'Blessed are the peace-makers.' Surely the last thing he would have wished was to be a party to controversy. Is that what you think? Well, if you do, I am sure that you will find John chapter 8 a nasty shock.

Here we find Jesus in the midst of a fiery altercation. John tells us that it all happened at the Feast of the Tabernacles, or Harvest Thanksgiving as we would call it. In fact chapters 7 and 8 of John really form a continuous record of the debate that was going on over that whole week of festivities. Big crowds had descended on Jerusalem to celebrate the holiday. As usual there was plenty of gossip flying around. But this year, John tells us one topic was dominating everybody's conversation: Jesus.

At first everyone was spreading rumours about whether he would dare to come down to the feast at all, especially since the last time he had been in Jerusalem, the authorities had sought his life. But then halfway through the festivities their speculations on this point were answered. Suddenly Jesus was in the midst, teaching in the very Temple precincts.

Immediately the subterranean smoulderings of debate about him erupted into volcanic action. Some began to take his side. He is a good man, they said; perhaps even the Messiah. But others, particularly amongst the Jewish establishment, became more and more militant in their antagonism towards him. John tells us in chapter 7 that before the week was out they had made several attempts to arrest Jesus. But such was the strength of his public support and the power of his personal charisma that the guards they sent just lacked the nerve to carry out their orders.

So as time went on a direct confrontation between Jesus and these leading Jews became practically inevitable. At length, on the final day of the holiday, Jesus stood up and spoke to the crowds one last time.

> I am the light of the world. Whoever follows me will never walk in darkness, but will have the light of life (8:12).

It was a very appropriate metaphor. During the Feast of Tabernacles, the Temple courtyard where people presented their harvest gifts was illuminated by huge chandeliers, symbolising perhaps the pillar of fire that had guided the Israelites during their wilderness wanderings. John tells us in 8:20 that Jesus delivered his final speech standing precisely in this very part of the Temple. So it may well have been just as these giant festival lights were being extinguished and dismantled that he offered himself to the departing multitudes as an alternative illumination. 'Follow me,' he says, 'and you'll find your way out of the darkness of your directionless existence. I am the light of the world. Just as the pillar of fire guided your forefathers to the promised land, I can guide you to life.'

It was a huge claim; but as we have seen, earlier in this book, it was in every way typical of Jesus. For the Jewish hierarchy, it was clearly the last straw. They felt they just had to take some action to deflate the popularity of this dangerous megalomaniac. So, with the prestigious Pharisees leading the attack, they launched a public assault on his credibility. 'You can't say that,' they argued. 'You're appearing as your own witness. Your testimony is not valid.'

Now a representative of our liberal, tolerant, undogmatic twentieth century would have listened very politely to their objections and sought some conciliatory form of words with which to defuse the situation. 'Why don't we all go to arbitration and sort these things out, brothers.' But what I want you to notice is that Jesus in this passage does nothing of that sort. Far from appeasing them, he repudiates their criticisms and, turning defence into attack, vehemently challenges them in return. If what follows is not to be called a controversy, I do not know what is.

The Jews cast veiled aspersions on the legitimacy of Jesus' birth, and some very direct aspersions on the sanity of his mind. 'Where is your father?' they asked sneeringly. 'We were not born out of wedlock. Aren't we right in saying that you are one of those mongrel half-breed Samaritans?

And demon-possessed to boot!' But if we are going to be honest we have to say that Jesus, for his part, gives as good as he gets in this exchange of verbal fireworks. He calls them liars and would-be murderers. He even calls them children of the devil.

All of which, of course, causes some embarrassment to our modern, liberal commentators on the passage. Such language is surely not really consistent with the doctrine of the universal brotherhood of man. I suppose it is just possible to accept one scholar's suggestion and envisage Jesus calling his opponents all these rude names, but with a consistently benign and loving expression on his face! But such a view stretches my imagination to breaking point.

It is certainly important to note that it is Jesus' opponents and not he himself who, at the end of the debate, introduce the element of physical violence by picking up stones to pelt him. On the other hand, it must be said that Jesus does nothing to placate this rising hostility in them. On the contrary, his attitude throughout seems almost calculated to provoke it. Agreeable as it would be to portray Jesus as one of your liberal, tolerant, ecumenical theologians of the twentieth century, I do not think the cap fits. Jesus was a controversialist.

Indeed it is one of the central purposes of John's gospel to map the growing bitterness of that controversy in which he was involved as it inexorably accelerates during the final year of his public ministry to its bloody finale on the cross. Chapter 8 is in many respects a critical point in this escalation towards violence. For our purposes in this study, we will concentrate on verses 31–35, at the centre of the controversy.

What Jesus says about Truth

To the Jews who had believed him, Jesus said, 'If you hold to my teaching, you are really my disciples. Then you will know the Truth . . . .' (8:31–32).

I find something particularly compelling about that phrase, 'You will know the truth.' All through history men have been convinced that behind the complexity and variety of the universe there must lie some absolute and unitary principle of order and coherence. We feel intuitively that must be the case. In the East this 'Truth' has been interpreted religiously in terms of a spiritual force which man discovers through mystical experience. In the West it has been interpreted, at least in recent times, in scientific terms; as a mathematical or physical principle, which man discovers through his own intellectual efforts.

It is fascinating to observe that one consequence of the contemporary rapprochement between Eastern and Western thought is that a synthesis is developing between these scientific and mystical approaches to Truth. For instance, in *Star Wars* you find Luke Skywalker seeking Buddhist enlightenment in between adventuring in his high technology space ship. Such is the irony of New Age thinking!

But so far as our passage here is concerned, the important thing to notice is that Jesus is overturning both Western and Eastern presuppositions in this quest for Truth. He has nothing to do with either of them. 'Real Truth,' he says, 'is neither a mystical force nor a mathematical formula. Ultimate reality is a relationship with a person; with me in fact. If you hold to my teaching, if you are really my disciples, then you will know the Truth.'

In other words, Truth is not something that you experience through yoga or discover through science, it is Someone to be encountered and followed. 'Commit yourselves to me,' he says, 'and you will know the Truth for which you are searching. In fact if you did but know it, when you look behind this universe for some great unchanging and abiding principle of coherence, you are looking for me.' As he would say to his disciples a little later, 'I am the Truth.' That claim is a really momentous one, and it has some very important implications for us.

First of all, it exposes the fallacy of those who think you can only become a Christian by committing intellectual suicide. Faith, they claim, is a blind leap in the dark. It is not an act of reason, but of desperation. As the schoolboy wrote in his RE exam, 'Faith is believing what you know ain't true.' I cannot find words sufficiently strong to repudiate that nonsense. Jesus says here that we do not give up the quest for Truth and receive him instead. It is as the Truth that Jesus wants to be accepted, or not at all. Indeed because he is the source of all truth, he is far more concerned about our intellectual integrity in receiving him than we are ourselves. He wants a discipleship that is motivated by the quest for Truth, not by a flight from it.

Secondly, we can see here why it is that mere intellectualism is never going to satisfy any human being's longing for Truth. It is for the simple reason that Truth is not an idea which we must conceptualise, but a Person with whom we must become involved. Maybe you are a mathematician, dreaming that one day you will win the Nobel Prize for being the first person to complete the unified field theory. You are going to integrate all known physical phenomena in one set of equations that will thereafter be known by your name.

Suppose you succeed in that ambition. Do you think that when you have fulfilled your dream you will know the Truth? No, all you will have done is to find out a little more precisely how the universe behaves. But the answer to the question *why* there is a universe at all would be as incomprehensible to you as ever. Answers to the question 'how' may be describable by your higher mathematics, but answers to the question 'why' are, according to Jesus, discoverable only by Christian discipleship.

That is why there are many humble, non-intellectual souls in this world who can barely recall their two times table but who may be incomparably closer to the Truth than you are, in spite of your knowledge of general relativity and quantum mechanics.

The third thing that we learn here is why it is utterly pointless either to demand or to attempt to give scientific proofs of the Christian message. You constantly find people who are trying to do so. 'Prove it to me,' they ask. Sometimes they are looking for logical demonstrations, a list of mathematical symbols with 'QED' at the bottom. Sometimes they are searching for miraculous demonstrations. 'All right God, if you are there, write it in the sky: I'm here, OK? Yours truly, Jesus.' But either way, the logic is always the same. 'I won't believe *unless* . . .' They put a conditional clause on their discipleship—'I'll follow Jesus, *if* you prove to me it's true.'

But it cannot be done. Such people want to put the cart before the horse. Christianity cannot be proved first and practised afterwards. According to Jesus, the proof is dependent on the practice, which is why he puts the conditional clause the other way round. He doesn't say, '*If* it's the Truth, follow my teaching.' He says, '*If* you follow my teaching, you will know the Truth.'

There is a splendid example of this in Rebecca Manley Pippert's book, *Out of the Saltshaker* (IVP). She tells the story of Sue. Sue was a very bright student, but an agnostic. She was interested in Christianity but had many intellectual questions about faith. So she came to Rebecca and told her 'I'm plagued with doubts. I can't pray to receive Christ because it would be dishonest. What should I do?' So Rebecca advised her, 'Tell God, or the four walls if that's what you think you are speaking to, that you want to find out if Jesus is truly God, and that if you could feel more certain you would follow him. Then begin to read the gospels, every day. Each day as you read, something will probably hit you and make sense. Whatever that is, do it as soon as you can.'

Sue gulped and replied, 'That's radical. But I'll do it.' So she started having what she called 'pagan quiet times', praying to the walls and then reading her Bible.

This is what happened:

One day, I read in the Bible, 'If someone steals your coat, don't let him have only that, but offer your cloak as well.' For whatever reason, that verse hit me between the eyes. So I said to the four walls, 'Listen walls—or God if you're there—I'm going to do what this verse says if the opportunity arises today. I want to remind you that I am trying to do things your way in order to find out if you exist and if Jesus really is who he says. Amen.'

The day went by and I forgot the verse. Then I headed to the library to continue working on my senior thesis. Just as I sat down at my designated thesis desk this guy comes up and starts yelling at me. He told me the school hadn't given him his thesis desk so he was going to take mine . . . I started yelling back aud pretty soon we caused quite a ruckus. It was when he glared at me and said, 'Look I'm stealing it from you whether you like it or not,' that it suddenly hit me.

I just looked at him and moaned. OHHHHH, no. I can't believe it . . . 'Look God, if you're there, I do want to know if Jesus is God. But isn't there some other way of finding out besides obeying that verse? I mean, couldn't I tithe or get baptised or give up something else? But DON'T TAKE MY THESIS DESK! I mean with my luck I'll give up the desk and then discover that you don't exist.'

But I couldn't escape the fact that I had read the verse the very same day that someone tried to rob me. Before, I'd always been amused to see how Jesus aimed for the jugular vein in his conversations with people in the Bible. But now it didn't feel so funny. I took a deep breath, tried not to swear and said, 'OK, you can have the desk.'

He looked bewildered . . . he grabbed my arm and asked me why in the world was I going to let him have it. I told him he would think I'd really flipped out, but I was trying to discover if Jesus was really who he claimed to be. I was attempting to do the things he told us to do. 'And today I read that if somebody tried to rip me off I was supposed to let them and even throw in something extra to boot.' All I could see were the whites of his eyes. 'So I'm going to give you the desk but don't press your luck about the something extra.' Then he asked, 'Why in the world would Jesus say such a crazy thing?' Then I said, 'Hey, if there's one thing I've learned from reading about Jesus and meeting some real Christians, it's that Jesus would give you a whole lot more than a thesis desk if you'd let him. I know Jesus would give it to you. So that thesis desk is yours.'

And this is the sentence I want you to think about:

> As I said those words *I just simply knew it was all true.* I kinda felt like God was saying, 'Well done. That's the way I want my children to behave.' (*Out of the Saltshaker*, IVP, pages 98–100.)

That is exactly what Jesus is saying here. 'If you hold to my teaching, you are really my disciples and you will know the Truth.' It is rather like marriage. You may think you know what marriage is like before you commit yourself to it, but you don't. You don't know the half, because marriage involves a personal relationship. Jesus says that Truth is the same. You cannot discover it without commitment to the person concerned.

To put it another way, you cannot approach Jesus on the lines of purely theoretical analysis. Your interest in him has to be experimental from the beginning or you will never get anywhere. Jesus is making a remarkable promise. He says here that without reading tomes of philosophy, or mastering Boolean algebra, or practising yoga meditation techniques, you and I can touch the ultimate reality behind the universe. In the daily routine of living we can find our existence becoming integrated and meaningful. Instead of going nowhere, we shall find we are going somewhere. Instead of feeling alienated we shall feel we belong, that we know who we are, why we are here and where we are going.

We can know what the world is for and why we are in it. We can know the Truth, and through nothing more complicated than placing our faith in him and proving our commitment to him by our adhering to his teaching.

What Jesus says about Freedom

> . . . you will know the truth, and the truth will set you free. They answered him, 'We are Abraham's descendents and have never been slaves of anyone' (8:32–33).

If there is one thing that has generated as much or more human motivation in history than the quest for Truth, it is the quest for Freedom. For most of us the word immediately evokes political associations. We think of the many thousands of people who fought and died to emancipate themselves from dictatorial régimes. Think of the French Revolution and its street cry of 'liberté'. Or of Franklin D. Roosevelt's famous fourfold definition of freedom in his speech to Congress in 1941: freedom of speech, freedom of worship, freedom from want, freedom from fear. Freedom, according to Roosevelt, was something that you had to achieve through democratic government and social justice, which is the way that most of us think about it today.

Though the Jews of Jesus' day would not have expressed it in quite the same way, they were basically thinking along political lines too. 'What do you mean?' they asked. 'We are Abraham's descendents and have never been slaves of anyone. How can you say we shall be set free? That future tense is out of place, Jesus. We're Israelites! Slavery is anathema to us.' To be honest, their retort was a little optimistic, because like countless others at that particular time they were part of the Roman Empire. But the Jews had noble thoughts, as they always have done. They did not think of themselves as slaves, even if other people did.

But it is not for that reason that Jesus talks about a need

for freedom. In fact the vital thing to notice about what he says here is that when he speaks of freedom, his mind is not on political liberation at all.

I tell you the truth. Everyone who sins is a slave to sin (8:34).

In other words, in Jesus' mind the most vicious form of bondage to which we human beings are victim is not bondage to oppressive political systems at all. The fundamental slavery of the human race, he says, is slavery to moral failure—to sin. It is the evil habits we cannot break, the selfish desires we must gratify and the shameful guilt we are unable to escape which are our real masters.

While we serve them all, proud talk about political freedom is just so much empty cant. Freedom of speech you may have, but control of your tongue you do not. Freedom of worship you may have, but love for God in your heart you do not. Freedom from want you may have, but contentment with what you have, you do not. You may be free from fear, but you do not enjoy peace of conscience. What is more, Jesus teaches, even if you were to admit to yourself the seriousness of your bondage to moral failure, you could not do anything to emancipate yourself from it. Since you are a slave, your position is one of powerlessness in the moral realm.

A slave has no permanent place in the family. But a son belongs to it for ever (8:35).

There is only one person in the universe, says Jesus, who can liberate you from the servitude to which you are so inextricably victim. That is someone who does not share your captivity. Only the person who can say, 'Can any of you prove me guilty of sin?' (v.46) or 'I always do what pleases [God]' (v.29) can also say:

So if the Son sets you free, you will be free indeed (8:36).

Once again Jesus is making some huge claims in these words. First of all, it makes absolutely clear to us why it was Jesus refused to be a political messiah. As we saw in John 6, his Galilean fellow countrymen were very enthusiastic about making him king of their anti-imperialist liberation army. But Jesus declined their offer. His reason is now obvious. Political liberation was not his mission. He had something far more important to do in the way of deliverance than merely the emancipation of men and women from their political oppressors. He was here to do something about the dominion of sin over human lives.

In his eyes it was that which ruined the world, and it succeeds in doing so no matter who holds the reins of power. That is why no matter how many revolutions you have, in ninety-nine cases out of a hundred you finish up with another dictator ten times worse than the one you got rid of. The philosopher Jean-Jacques Rousseau said that man was born free and it was society that put him in chains; Jesus says that is not the case at all. We are *born* in chains. That is the measure of our helplessness.

That is why, of course, the extreme Left will always be made up of very young men and women. It has to be so, because only those who are young enough not to have been disillusioned by the inveteracy of evil in this world will be capable of the necessary utopianism about the human race. Old men have learned by bitter experience to be cynical about the perfectability of humanity. There was some famous correspondence in *The Times* at the turn of the century. The newspaper asked for people's opinion of what was wrong with the world. Predictably, there were all kinds of letters, some of which blamed the system, some education and some the government. The letter from author G.K. Chesterton was however very short. It simply said, 'Dear Sir, I am. Yours faithfully, G.K. Chesterton.'

That is the truth to which Jesus is trying to point us here, namely, that *we* are the problem with the world. You want to understand what is wrong with the world? Look in the mirror! I remember a Marxist student once told me with great glee about the marvellous classless society that socialism would one day set up. So I asked him, 'Are you sure that when this marvellous classless society appears, you won't spoil it?' As Golding demonstrates in his book, *Lord of the Flies,* evil is not some superficial rash on the surface of the human race, born of our capitalistic economics, or our bourgeois education. It is a moral cancer that eats at the heart of every individual member of the human race. No matter how young we may be, or how idyllic our environment, evil will out. You can call Jesus a reactionary if you will. I prefer to call him a realist. If this world is going to be changed, he says, it is not radically new politics we need. It is radically new people. And that is what Jesus is offering: 'The Son can make you free.'

That brings us to the second thing which this passage makes very clear: the difference between real Freedom and that with which it is often confused these days: permissiveness. The 1960s coined the phrase the 'permissive society'. Of course, when people used it, they did not mean that the 1960s were a deeper den of vice than any era that had preceded them. What made the sixties different was that freedom became radically re-interpreted. For the first time, really large numbers of ordinary people began to define freedom as the liberty to do as you want. Moral values, they said, were just social conventions.

Of course, scholars had been saying things like that for a long time; but this was the first time that such a view gained widespread popular credence. To be really free, it was argued, we had to be willing to defy the inhibiting influence which social conventions had over us. We must add to Roosevelt's famous four freedoms a fifth; freedom of choice, freedom to 'Do your own thing', to be your own person. It is a very intoxicating thought. But according to Jesus it is utterly wrong. Devising a new morality no more liberates men and women than creating a new political order does.

You see, moral values are built into this universe by the moral God who made both it and us. When we sin, therefore, we are not just flouting social conventions that men have invented. We are like elephants trying to fly. We are defying laws which we have been made by nature to obey. That is why Jesus says that anybody who sins is a slave to sin.

There is a story from Australia which illustrates the point a little. A snake managed to enter a home one day and saw a canary in a cage. It decided that the bird would make a tasty morsel, and so went through the bars of the cage and ate it. Unfortunately once the bird was in its throat, the snake was too big to get back out of the cage again. It was 'a prisoner of appetite'! To me, that is a model of what the human race has done. We have refused to accept the moral limits which the Creator has placed upon us. Determined to find our way through the bars, we now find ourselves not free at all, but imprisoned. All our so-called permissiveness has brought us is a miserable bondage to self-indulgence.

True freedom is not liberty to do as you want. That is licence, or anarchy. True freedom is the liberty to do as you *ought*. It involves the recognition that we are not here simply to 'do our own thing'. We are here as sons and daughters of God, to live our lives in accordance with our Maker's plan. He gives us huge liberty to enjoy. Those no-entry signs which are there are displayed not to spoil our fun, but to protect our Freedom. Jesus would show us that true Freedom. He wants to re-introduce it to us, and he can do it, for he possesses the key to the cage. He is the Son. If the Son makes you free you will be free indeed.

What Jesus says about himself

[Jesus said] 'You are from below; I am from above. You are of

this world; I am not of this world. I told you that you would die
in your sins; if you do not believe that I am the one I claim to
be, you will indeed die in your sins' (8:23–24).

When Jesus offers men and women liberating truth, it is
never an optional extra. So far as he is concerned it is not
the icing on the cake of life. It is a vital necessity. Without
this liberating truth we will die in our sins. For most of us,
the thought of dying is bad enough, but not for Jesus. He
could say, 'I tell you the truth, if a man keeps my word, he
will never see death' (v.51). In other words, death will pass
by like a bridge on a train journey, so innocuous as hardly
to be noticed.

It is no terrible thing to die. But it is a terrible thing to die
in your sins, to die unliberated by the Truth that is in Jesus,
with the weight of guilt and shame still like a noose round
your neck and face the judgement of the God who made us.
But 'unless people believe in the unique Person that I am,'
says Jesus, 'that will be their destiny.'

Now do you see why Jesus was so controversial? He does
not engage in controversy just for the fun of it. He was
naturally of an irenical spirit. If Jesus gets so excited about
those who deny his claims, you can be sure that absolutely
vital issues are at stake. So we must not be seduced by the
bland assurances of liberal twentieth-century theologians
who tell us that everything will be all right for everybody in
the end. Certainly, Jesus is the light of the whole world. But
Jesus was not a universalist. He did not believe that everybody was going to heaven. In fact, in his own way the faith
he brought was every bit as exclusive, as narrow, yes even
as intolerant as the Judaism which it supplanted.

For Jesus did not believe that the truth lay in all great
religions, or that men could find freedom anywhere and
everywhere they wanted. He insisted that Truth and Freedom came from him, and him alone. 'I am the light of the
world,' he said. The emphasis in that verse falls not on the

universality of the word 'world' but on the exclusiveness of
the pronoun 'I'. Photographers know that one of the things
light does is to cast shadows, thereby creating contrasts.
The more intense and the more uni-directional the light is,
the deeper those shadows, and the starker those contrasts.
So Jesus as the light of the world did not come to dispel controversy. His purpose was to dwarf all previous controversies into insignificance by the polarising effects of his own
person. Of course he had to be a controversialist! The
issues at stake were far too serious, much too far-reaching
to be weak-kneed about them. 'If you don't believe that I
am he,' he said, 'you will die in your sins'.

As he spoke those very words, the spectators in the
crowd were being ever more sharply divided. The contrast
was appearing: for him or against him. And it will be so for
some of you reading this. Some of you will turn your face
towards the light, and others of you will turn your back to it.
Of the former, he says, 'If you hold to my teaching, and
stick to it, you will really be my disciples. You will know the
truth and the truth will set you free.' The proof of the pud-
ding is in the eating. To the latter he says, 'Why is my language unclear? It is because you are unable to hear what I
say. You are of your father the devil.' Is it not a terrible
thing to be numbered with those who crucified Jesus?

And to those of you who are still sitting in the twilight
zone, between light and darkness, he issues this solemn
warning: 'If you do not believe that I am the One I claim to
be, you will indeed die in your sins.' There is no decision
any human being can make which is of greater importance
than that. That is why Jesus had to be a controversialist.
That is why those who follow him may sometimes have to
be controversialists too.

6

The Shepherd

John 10:1–42

Heaven as conventionally conceived is a place so inane, so dull, so useless, so miserable that nobody has ever ventured to describe a whole day there, though plenty of people have described a day at the seaside. *(Misalliance [or Parents and Children]* Constable, 1914.)

That is George Bernard Shaw in the preface to one of his plays, expressing a sentiment with which I confess I have some sympathy. Heaven in most people's minds, I fear, is not a particularly inviting place. Indeed as a child I can distinctly remember being deeply apprehensive at the prospect of going there.

'What do you do there?' I asked. 'It will be so boring!' Part of the trouble was that my infantile image of heaven was largely shaped by the Gothic architecture of the local parish church. It was, I recall, a place associated in my mind with interminable dreariness and hard pews on which one was not permitted to fidget. However, as I reflect a bit more deeply, I realise that my reservations about heaven actually go rather deeper than that. It was not simply the austerity of St Michael and All Angels on the corner of the High Street that was to blame. I had as a child a distinct uneasiness with the whole concept of eternity generally. Whenever I asked people what eternity was, they always told me that it means 'living for ever and ever, dear.'

Frankly I found such an idea quite appalling. It was hard

enough to keep myself amused during the six weeks of the school summer holiday. To have to do so for years and years on end, by my reckoning, was no recipe for perpetual bliss but rather one for perpetual tedium. Indeed, if heaven really was anything like St Michael and All Angels, there would not even be any toys to play with up there—just a monotonous droning of the organ, not to mention the Vicar. No, George Bernard Shaw was quite right. Give me a day at the seaside any time in preference to heaven!

I sometimes wonder whether, underneath the intellectual objections that many sceptics raise to the Christian faith these days, there does not lie a very similar disquiet, albeit a subconscious one. Certainly, when I talk to many young people outside the church I often come away feeling that they have rejected Christianity not because they are strongly convinced that it's false, but simply because the distinct impression has been given to them that it is dull.

It is a very great pity, because as I realise now, it is all founded on a tragic misconception. The idea of living for ever and ever is not only a very inadequate description of heaven, but also a positively sub-Christian one. Spiritualists may be satisfied with simply surviving beyond the grave. But Christians are not! Even the ancient Greeks perceived that mere immortality would not be a blessing for the human race but a curse. Jesus, however, never offered mere immortality. Notice what he says:

> I have come that they may have life, aud have it to the full (10:10).

Heaven for Jesus was not an extension of the duration of life, but an intensification of the experience of life. Jesus did not come merely to offer us more life quantitatively, but more life qualitatively—'life to the full'.

I do not know much about heaven. Nobody does. But I can guarantee one thing. Nobody there is ever bored. I doubt whether anybody in heaven ever thinks so much as to look at their watch. Have you not sometimes had, for a fleeting moment or two, such an experience? As a student perhaps, when you sat up late talking about things with your college friends, just talking and talking. The hours flew by but you were never conscious of their passing, because there was a kind of glow inside you generated by the companionship which you were experiencing. You never wanted the evening to end. That is what heaven is like—'life to the full'.

Or perhaps some of you have felt that thrill, that very sublime rapture, when reading a great book, or watching a great play, or listening to great music; as if joy had so totally enthralled you that it lifted you for that moment out of time and space altogether. Have you ever felt that? That is what heaven is like, 'life to the full'.

Or maybe you have climbed a mountain in the early morning and stood there on the summit, captivated by the grandeur of the scene. You felt that you could stand there for ever, and never grow tired of looking at it. Or maybe you have fallen in love, and know that very peculiar euphoria at the prospect of seeing him or her once again. 'I was just existing till I met you,' we say. That too is what heaven is like—'life to the full'!

Forget about the Gothic architecture, about the hard pews. Take the deepest enchantment that you have ever known, the loftiest ecstasy that you have ever felt. Take the greatest fulfilment you have ever experienced. Take that moment when you felt most totally alive. Then intensify that instant a millionfold, and perhaps you will be getting within range of imagining what heaven is like. Jesus did not come to give us more time to kill. He came to give us more life to live. 'I have come that they may have life and have it to the full.'

Some of you may find that difficult to believe. I respect your incredulity, though I would like to have the opportunity to change it. But if any of you says he finds that too dull to interest him, or too unattractive to be worth investigating, I am at a loss to imagine what you *would* consider exciting or important.

Jesus has come to offer us life to the full. We need to discover three vital things about that life if we are going to enjoy it as Jesus wants us to. They come out of the parable of pastoral life which Jesus first tells us, in John chapter 10, and then progressively interprets to us.

The source of life

> I tell you the truth, the man who does not enter the sheep pen by the gate, but climbs in by some other way, is a thief and a robber (10:1).

They did not possess bank vaults in Jesus' day. Their wealth was measured in cattle or sheep, not in pieces of coloured paper. But security against theft was of course still very important. So every town and village had the equivalent of a bank, namely the sheep pen; an enclosed space where the animals could be looked after, with high walls and a gate. Beside the gate or perhaps even lying down in its entrance was a guard.

Bona fide shepherds would of course recognise the watchman and be recognised by him. They would be allowed through the gate to summon their flock. On the other hand, anyone who tried to climb over the walls to get in was obviously up to no good. They were out to steal the sheep or to slaughter them. As Jesus puts it, they were thieves and robbers (the word 'robber' had the additional connotation of violence as well as larceny). So everybody in Jesus' audience knew exactly what he meant when he said that the only legitimate way into the sheep pen was through the gate.

> I am the gate for the sheep. All who ever came before me were thieves and robbers, but the sheep did not listen to them. I am

the gate; whoever enters through me will be saved (10:7–9).

This is another one of those startling and very emphatic statements to which we have grown accustomed in these discourses in John's gospel. Notice once again the emphasis on the first person singular pronoun. '*I* am the gate.' Jesus is distinguishing himself here, very forcibly, from certain others whom he derogates not just as rivals but as criminals, 'thieves and robbers'. In order to understand what he is talking about, we first have to identify who these others are.

There are two possibilities. The first is that Jesus is referring here to the Jewish establishment of his own day. If you look back at previous chapters you will see that this discourse in chapter 10 follows straight on from the controversy which Jesus had begun to have with the high-ranking Jews (we looked at that in the previous chapter of this book). In fact at the very end of chapter 9 we find Jesus contradicting the Pharisees in a very outspoken way, telling them that they are not really competent to lead others because they are spiritually blind. And he says that their refusal to admit their spiritual blindness renders them all the more culpable.

So it is tempting to identify the thieves and robbers that Jesus goes on to describe immediately in 10:1 as these Pharisees and others like them. Jesus was saying that they were not the true shepherds of God's flock, though they claimed to be. They were, in fact, just vandals causing irreparable damage to God's sheep. There are many commentators who pursue that line of interpretation through these verses.

But there is a serious flaw, to my mind, in that theory, and it is revealed by Jesus' comment in verse 8, 'All who ever came before me.' That seems a very unnatural way to speak of the Jewish establishment. Firstly, they were not Jesus' predecessors, but his contemporaries. So why does he talk about them coming before him? Secondly, because of the comprehensiveness of the word *all*. What about Nicodemus and the others of whom we read among the Jewish aristocracy putting their faith in Jesus contrary to the general trend among their peers? Jesus was surely not offering a blanket condemnation of every priest and scribe who had ever exerted influence on the Jewish people.

It seems to me that the only way in which we can make sense of what Jesus says in verse 8 is to say that in fact it was not the Jewish establishment at all that was in his mind here, but someone else. He is referring in fact to the false messiahs who had arisen in Israel and with whom he was constantly in danger of being confused by the people at large. We know from other first-century historical sources that there were many such charismatic leaders in the century or so immediately preceding Jesus' ministry. Indeed Galilee, his own home area, was notorious as a seed-bed for their movements.

It is not surprising that Jesus alludes to them, for John seems to have a special interest in demonstrating to his readership the radical distinction between these political activists, who were so common and so well-known to the people of his day, and Jesus. We have noticed several references to that already, especially in chapter 6 when Jesus rejected the invitation of the Galilean mob to be their king. This is one more example of the evangelist's concern to show us that Jesus was not a political messiah.

The imagery of thieves and robbers was of course much more obviously applicable to these self-styled saviours of Israel than it was to the Jewish establishment. They were, without exception, men of violence. They sought to free Israel from the yoke of imperial Rome by revolution. We would call them freedom-fighters, or even terrorists.

Whatever moral verdict you pass on their activities, the important thing so far as Jesus was concerned is that they exploited the messianic expectations of the people. 'Once we have thrown out the Romans,' they said, 'then the new age of peace and plenty that the prophets talk about in the Old Testament will finally dawn.' Some of them in fact made quite personal claims to be the messiah. They did not say they were just shepherds, in the general sense of being national leaders. They arrogated to themselves the title *The* Shepherd. This was the messianic title used by Ezekiel in the Old Testament when God said through him 'I will save my flock [Israel] . . . . And I will place over them one shepherd, my servant David, and he will tend them and be their Shepherd' (Ezek 34:22–23).

So when Jesus says 'All who ever came before me are thieves and robbers,' he is saying very emphatically that without exception, all those who had claimed such messianic titles in the past had been impostors. Their violent methods, he says, were in themselves evidence of their imposture. 'I am the gate. I am the only One who has the right to be called the Christ, the Messiah. The way to the promised kingdom of heaven is through me, and through absolutely nobody else.'

If we are right in detecting this allusion to the revolutionary movements of the first century in these verses, it means of course that this passage has a very direct and important relevance to our twentieth-century situation. For the only real hope for the future which modern man can embrace, in his disaffection with the traditional Christian idea of heaven, is some kind of alternative humanistic utopia.

The classic expression of that derives from the genius of Karl Marx, as embodied in his classless society. In many respects this is just a secularised vision of heaven. Marx said that people can only discover their true happiness or fulfilment, once they have liberated themselves from economic oppression and exploitation and discovered in the collapse of the capitalist system the bliss of participating in a paradise on earth. In such a state, all the old alienations would be dissolved and man would be free to develop his full human potential.

That is the Marxist dream, and it is a very powerful one. There clearly are grave weaknesses in the capitalist system. It is very tempting for us to blame all our frustrations and misery in life upon its victimisation of us. Yet, in a very real sense, that was precisely what these false messiahs in Jesus' day were saying too. It was imperialism, they said, that was the problem. If they could only overthrow the Romans then the kingdom of God would arrive. Notice the response which Jesus makes to that—it is an emphatic 'no'. 'Do not be duped by these messiahs of violence,' he says. 'They are not saviours at all, but brigands.' See the hallmark of their stock in trade. A blatant disregard for personal property— 'They come to steal'. A ruthless indifference to human life—'They come to kill'. An irrational contempt for anything of value—'They come to destroy'.

Two thousand years have not changed the pattern. This trio of criminality has been characteristic of every revolutionary movement the world has seen, not least the Marxist variety. I know that we often cite the appalling genocide of Hitler against the Jews as a symbol of the degree to which man's inhumanity to man can go. Yet the cold statistical truth is that compared to the vast millions who have perished under Lenin, under Stalin, under Mao, under Pol Pot, in our century, the death toll of fascist Germany seems almost modest.

What has been achieved by all this hideous carnage and revolutionary violence? Where is this perfect society of which Marx dreamed? Did they find it in Soviet Russia? Or is it in China? No, Jesus is right. It is not the Christian doctrine of heaven that is the myth, but the humanist dream of utopia. That is the thing which never materialises. Of course, revolutions do accomplish something every now and then. Jesus is not such a fool as to forget that the life of his nation had occasionally benefited from a *coup d'état*. He would, however, have us realise two very important things here.

Firstly, whatever revolutions achieve they do so only at the expense of much property, many lives and incalculable destruction of culture. The thief comes to steal and to kill and to destroy. Secondly, and more significantly, whatever these revolutions achieve, they never bring to human beings that new quality of fulfilment in life that their ideological messiahs promised. 'I am the gate,' said Jesus. He, and nobody else, had come that they might have life. People who go his way are the ones who will find true liberty. 'They go in and they go out.' They are the ones who find true deliverance. 'They are saved.' They are the ones who find true fulfilment. 'They find pasture.' A man must enter by Christ if he wants to find real liberation, real satisfaction, real life. 'I am the gate.' And note very carefully, he doesn't carry a machine gun. He carries a cross.

The cost of life

I am the good Shepherd. The good Shepherd lays down his life for the sheep (10:11).

It is important to realise that the phrase 'good shepherd' would not generate the kind of sentimentality in a Jew which I suspect it does in us. For some reason, in English culture shepherds are viewed as rather romantic figures who spend most of their time cuddling little lambs and roaming hillsides with their faithful dogs. That was not the image which a shepherd had in Israel. They were men who lived dangerous lives.

Even more important than that, however, as we have already noted when 'shepherd' was used with the definite article ('*the* Shepherd') by somebody like Jesus, it had a messianic significance. It evoked feelings not so much of sentimentality but of royalty. That is why Jesus' audience was thrown into such a state of bewilderment. If he had said, 'I am the Shepherd come to lead Israel to freedom,' there is not one of them who would have missed what he was talking about. But Jesus did not. Instead, he insisted on welding this messianic metaphor of the Shepherd on to the thought of death. Jesus' messiahship was not going to be like that of the impostors who had come before him. Their messiahship had taken the lives of men. Jesus' messiahship was going to give life to men, but only at the expense of his own.

There are three things about Jesus' death which he emphasises very clearly here. The first thing you will notice is that Jesus is quite convinced that his is going to be a *loving death*.

> The hired hand is not the shepherd who owns the sheep. So when he sees the wolf coming, he abandons the sheep and runs away. Then the wolf attacks the flock and scatters it. The man runs away because he is a hired hand and cares nothing for the sheep. I am the good shepherd, . . . I lay down my life for the sheep (10:12–15).

Of course, the word 'good' can mean various things. We can talk about a good car, if it works; we can talk about a good man, if he is morally upright. The interesting thing about the word 'good', which John uses here, is that it is not the normal one that you might associate either with efficiency or with moral uprightness. It is a word that has a distinct overtone of attractiveness. It often means 'good to look at'. Perhaps John is suggesting that people are not won to Jesus by the efficiency of his party machine, nor because they embrace his political ambitions but that it is the magnetism of his personal goodness that draws them to him. They are persuaded that he really cares for them.

Nowhere is this goodness seen better than in his willingness to die on their behalf. Of course there are those who appear to be shepherds, but are actually hired men, in it for what they can get out of it. They are motivated by self-interest and as a result, when you really need them you cannot rely on them because they are not really interested in you. They are just professional do-gooders. We have all met that kind of person. But Jesus is not like that. He is really concerned about us. He really wants us to enjoy fulfilment in life and he has proved it. If we had any doubt about it, he has demonstrated it conclusively by dying for us. Nowhere do we see the love in Christ's heart more clearly than there on the cross.

The second thing that I want you to notice is that it was also a *planned death*.

> No-one takes my life from me, but I lay it down of my own accord. I have authority to lay it down and authority to take it up again (10:18).

William Barclay tells the story of a young man in the First World War who was wounded in the trenches during an attack. The medic who came to treat him had to say to him, 'I'm sorry, soldier, you've lost your arm.' The young soldier is reputed to have replied, 'Doc, I didn't lose it. I gave it.' Jesus is saying something rather similar here. But he is not just saying that he came into this world willing to die, if necessary, like a soldier going into battle. He is stating that he came into this world knowing that death would be necessary. It was planned, and right through his life that plan was never thwarted. He was in control of his destiny all the time. He never saw himself as the tragic victim of circumstances. Such was his personal authority over events that he claims no one could take his life from him against his will. His death was a voluntary act of sacrifice, the most voluntary act of sacrifice of which any man has ever been capable. His life was not lost, but deliberately given.

That brings us to the third thing we have to notice if we are going to make sense of what Jesus is saying here: it was a *saving death*.

I know my sheep and my sheep know me . . . and I lay down
my life for the sheep (10:14–15).

What do you make of that? Some people suggest it means
that Jesus died to set the sheep an example of unselfishness.
A shepherd's death does of course prove that he is a very
unselfish person. As distinct from the hired hand, he has a
personal interest and care for the sheep. Otherwise he
would not have died.

But what sense does it make to say that the shepherd dies
in order to set the sheep an example? Suppose you were a
sheep, out in the wilderness somewhere and your shepherd
said to you, 'I love you sheep and I'm going to jump over
this cliff to prove it.' Can you make any sense out of that?
No! Even if sheep were more intelligent than they are usually supposed to be, they would be utterly bewildered. Only
in circumstances where the sheep were *in danger* would the
death of the shepherd make sense as an example of love.
That is the only possible situation that can arise where a
shepherd would die for his sheep as an intelligible act of
devotion to them.

One travelogue of the Middle East actually recounts
such an occasion, when a Semitic shepherd defended his
flock against three Bedouin robbers and was cut to pieces
in the act. That makes sense to us, as a demonstration of
love and dedication to the sheep. But jumping off a cliff
would not.

That is, of course, why Jesus has to mention the wolf.

When he sees the wolf coming [the hired hand] abandons the
sheep and runs away (10:12).

The reason many people have difficulty understanding
why Jesus had to die for them is because they do not realise
what danger they are in. It is as simple as that. There is a

wolf coming and Jesus knew it. Sinful men and women like us are one day going to die, and we will then have to face God in judgement. Jesus knew that was our situation and that it was an immensely perilous one.

Have you ever seen a sheep flock when there is a predator near, even when it is only a dog? They rush around in a completely futile panic. That is our human condition. We know we are doomed to die, and that knowledge mocks us. It starts mocking us from the very moment in our youth when we realise we are going to die one day. It continues mocking us through middle age and it goes on mocking us right up until the end. The wolf is coming! 'It is appointed to men once to die, and after death the judgement.' That is why we need a shepherd—the good Shepherd, not a professional do-gooder. We need the kind of shepherd who is willing to take our death from our shoulders and bear it himself. That is what Jesus means when he says that he is the good Shepherd and gives his life for the sheep. He did not give his life just to prove how much he loved us. He gave it to save us from the wolf.

The gift of life

> You do not believe because you are not my sheep. My sheep listen to my voice; I know them, and they follow me. I give them eternal life (10:26–27).

Jesus is doing here what we have seen him do so often in John's gospel, separating human beings into two groups. On the one hand, he says, there are some people who do not understand the cross. They do not understand Jesus. They do not realise how much danger they are in. They feel happy. They feel safe. They sense no wolf prowling around and so they feel no need of a shepherd to protect them. 'I'm OK,' they say. They do not believe in Jesus because they are not his sheep.

But, Jesus adds, there is another group and they feel

totally differently about things. They know their lives are empty and spoiled. And they desperately want to find that life in all its fullness that Jesus claims to provide. Such responsive men and women are not just a faceless multitude in Jesus' eyes. They are personally known to him. In a most intimate way, they belong to him. He calls them 'my sheep'. Is that the group which you belong to?

Jesus gives us here some very clear tests by which to know whether we are of that company.

My sheep listen to my voice (10:27).

They have heard other voices clamouring for their attention: the revolutionaries, the philosophers. All kinds of people have been saying 'Come my way'. But some kind of gut intuition has told them that all their claims are false, that their ideas are not going to meet the deep need of their hearts. They might dabble in them for a little while, but they quickly grow disillusioned. Eventually, they run away from those siren voices because they can hear another voice beckoning to them, a voice that compels their attention. They recognise it as the voice of the One who can really meet their need.

They follow me (10:27).

I like the way that Jesus puts it. Some people have the idea that when you become a Christian, Jesus shuts you in, puts you into a cage and takes away all your fun. It all goes back to what we were saying earlier about Christianity being dull.

But that is not the pattern as Jesus sees it. His sheep follow him *freely*. They are not coerced or whipped. They are not driven as though by a butcher. They follow voluntarily, because they know that is where their true freedom and true fulfilment lie. There may of course be some stupid sheep who prefer life in the sheep pen, or with one of those thieves and robbers, or even the hired hand. 'But,' says Jesus, 'my sheep know where they are well off. They follow me, and it's in following me that they discover that life which I have been talking about.'

That brings us to the third thing that marks out these sheep. They hear the voice of Jesus and recognise it for the authoritative voice that it is. They follow Jesus, changing their lives in order to be obedient to him. Then:

> I give them eternal life, and they shall never perish; no-one can snatch them out of my hand (10:28).

All around this world today there are people who are feeling insecure. They are not necessarily neurotic people, bowed down by their inadequate upbringings. They might be quite sane, well-adjusted people. But they still feel insecure, because they have no idea where they are going, or what they are here for. They do not really feel they belong, or that anybody loves them. They are cynical about life, about relationships, about careers, about just about everything, and at the root of that cynicism is insecurity.

What they need to feel is the reassurance of the Shepherd's hand. 'I give them eternal life,' says Jesus. 'It is a free gift to my sheep. They will never perish, and no one can ever remove them from the security of that new relationship they have with me. It is impossible. For it is my Father himself who has given them to me and he is greater than anything. His hand is invincible.'

There is a story I love about John Brown, the great Scottish pastor. He once visited a lady on her death-bed. 'Jane,' he said, 'what would you say if after all that he has done for you, God should let you perish?' The old woman thought for a moment and then she said, 'Well, if he did, he'd lose more than I would, I reckon. For I'd only lose my soul. He'd lose his honour, for he has said "they shall never perish".'

Dare I ask you whether you have heard the voice of the Shepherd? Dare I ask you whether, having heard it, you've followed him? That is what Jesus is calling us to. A life of discipleship; a life in that group who respond to his call. I cannot tell you where that life may lead you. It would be irresponsible of me to tell you that it will be a bed of roses, or that all the problems you are conscious of now will evaporate overnight. It is not going to be like that. Conversion is crossing a Rubicon. You might be in for anything. But one thing I do promise you. You will never find life with Jesus boring, even though it does last for ever.

7
The Way

John 13:36—14:14

There are very few experiences that are more distressing to the human heart than loss. Even if the object concerned is no more than a sentimental trinket or a pet animal, we still feel heartbroken. And when we lose a person, our sense of emotional devastation can be almost unendurable. Ask any widow, or orphan, or even a divorcee and they will tell you. Love's power to enrich our lives is matched only by its power to embitter them with tragedy when we lose what we have loved.

As we come to this final conversation in John's gospel, just such a tragedy is about to engulf the disciples. Judas has gone off into the night intent upon his act of betrayal. Jesus knew that it was now only a matter of hours before that moment arrived towards which his life had been inexorably moving for the last three years: the moment of his death.

The supper that he is sharing with his dear friends will be the last one they will have together. The premonition of that separation hangs dark and brooding like a pall over their whole conversation around the table. For their part, the disciples just cannot understand what's going on. They have never seen Jesus in this mood before. It bewilders and frightens them. Their hearts are troubled. Jesus speaks on the one hand of imminent triumph, 'Now is the Son of Man glorified.' But if that is so why does such dark sorrow furrow his brow? He challenges them with the importance of their mutual affection. 'Love one another,' he says. But why does he add that ominous past tense—'as I have loved you'?

Most disturbing of all, of course, is the way in which he keeps on echoing the depressing word 'going'. 'I am going,' he tells them. 'I'll be with you only a little longer, my children. You will look for me, but where I am going you cannot come.' In the same way that a dying parent tries to warn his little ones of the blow that is just about to strike their family, so Jesus here, with a tenderness almost unparalleled even within his gentle manners, prepares the disciples for his departure.

It is little wonder that this seventh and final discourse in John's gospel is often called the Farewell Discourse. No valedictory sermon ever preached is more moving or more sensitive. Many would judge that there is no passage in all the Scriptures that introduces Jesus quite so intimately. We shall look at just the first section of it, focusing our attention on three questions with which the disciples of Jesus, in their downcast and perplexed mood, respond to his air of gloomy foreboding. Each of the questions tells us something about the character of the enquirer and each represents a different kind of response to grief.

The question of Peter—the fanatic

> Simon Peter asked him, 'Lord, where are you going?'
> Jesus replied, 'Where I am going, you cannot follow now, but you will follow later.'
> Peter asked, 'Lord, why can't I follow you now? I will lay down my life for you' (13:36–37).

One often observes that the first stage of grief is simply nonacceptance, a refusal to believe the bad news. 'It can't be true, Doctor,' people say, 'there must be something you can do. I won't let it happen!'—and Peter, being an impetuous and excitable person, was an obvious candidate for that kind of semi-hysterical reaction. 'Why can't I follow you now?'

There is a kind of infantile petulance about his impatience. You can almost imagine him pouting as he says the words. The thought of separation had reduced this strong man to the self-pitying sulkiness of a whimpering child. We are not to blame him for that. Desperation in bereavement can very quickly reduce even the sanest of men to such irrational, immature protests. We dare not condemn him for his grief-stricken emotions. He was devoted to Christ.

Yet sympathy must not blind us to the peril implicit in his wild remarks either. 'I will lay down my life for you.' There is an irony there for, as we saw in the previous chapter, it was just a few months earlier that Jesus himself had used those very words. 'I am the good shepherd. The good shepherd lays down his life for the sheep.' Here Peter, consumed with love for his master, cannot bear such a thought. He would rather reverse the roles. 'No, Lord,' he is saying, 'you must not lay down your life for me. I will lay down my life for you!' I wonder if there was just a trace of an indulgent smile flickering on Jesus' lips, as he reflected this bravado back to Peter for a little maturer reflection? 'Will you?' he says. 'Will you really lay down your life for me?'

For all its veneer of self-abnegation, there are delusions of grandeur here. There is pride; fearless, courageous even admirable in some ways, but pride all the same, asserting its own individual superiority. He speaks not on behalf of the disciples but for himself alone. Though everybody else may be a craven coward, Peter will not be. 'I will lay down my life for you. It will be different for me, Jesus.'

'But, Peter,' says Jesus in effect, 'don't you realise that there are moments when you can do nothing? Nothing but be a spectator of somebody else's sacrifice? Nothing but be a recipient of somebody else's generosity? You cannot put me in your debt, Peter! It is impossible.' Jesus owes us nothing. It is we who depend on him for charity. Devastating as that may be for our egos, we have to get to the point where we are willing to see it that way. Pride is the one passion with which Jesus cannot allow any disciple of his to arrive at the dawn of Good Friday.

> I tell you the truth, before the cock crows, you will disown me three times! (13:38).

So Jesus answers the irony of Peter's boast with the even greater irony of Peter's denial. This brave disciple will, before the night is out, despise himself for his cowardice. This devoted disciple, before the dawn, will howl in self-reproach for his disloyalty. This superior disciple, before the night is out, will be blushing in shame at his failure. It will be a hard lesson to learn. But Peter must learn it, as indeed we all must learn it. For Jesus does not love us because we are faithful to him. He does not love us because we are willing to die for him. He loves us in spite of the fact that we are perfidious weaklings, and our devotion to him must be built on the embarrassment of that humiliating self-knowledge.

Maybe there are times when you feel that you have failed as a Christian. You have read missionary biographies and instead of inspiring you, they depress you in the extreme. 'Oh, if only I could be as committed as that,' you say to yourself. You go to your Bible study group and you come away feeling thoroughly inadequate. 'Oh, they are all so much keener than I am.' So you sit in a corner bowed down under your spiritual inferiority complex, dazzled by all the haloes that seem to be surrounding you.

Take heart. Jesus is not as impressed as you are by the veneer of super-spirituality which some of us project. He is a master psychiatrist, and he knows how much of it is just a defence-mechanism against our inner vulnerability. Wild gestures of discipleship, rash promises, intense Christian activity, crazy heroics: these are all the marks of a fanatic. And fanaticism is a neurosis, born not out of spiritual strength, but of chronic spiritual insecurity.

Jesus is not looking for fanaticism from you, any more than he was looking for it from Peter. The first thing he requires of any of us is *faith*.

> Do not let your hearts be troubled. Trust in God; trust also in me (14:1).

These famous words have cheered many a funeral in their time. But let it be noted, they were spoken first to a group of disciples who under the pressure of intense emotional battering were just about to fail. Jesus is encouraging them here, first and foremost, not to be cast down by that impending failure.

'Yes,' he is telling them, 'like Peter all of you, before the night is out, will feel like failures. But your infidelity will not forfeit your hope. This Christianity that I'm talking about is not based upon confidence in what you can do for me, but confidence in what I have done for you. Trust in me.'

> In my Father's house are many rooms; if it were not so, I would have told you. I am going there to prepare a place for you (14:2).

'Yes, even for you Peter, failure though you will shortly prove to be.'

That phrase 'many rooms' has led of course to a considerable amount of rather fanciful speculation on the part of commentators. Some, encouraged by the Authorised Version rendering of it as 'many mansions', have pictured each of the redeemed in heaven as furnished with some kind of spiritual equivalent of Buckingham Palace. Others have traced a connection to Jewish apocalyptic thought and believe that Jesus is talking here about degrees of bliss which the redeemed can enjoy in heaven; rather like on a luxury liner, with first-class, second-class and third-class berths. Still others point out that the Greek word used is employed by some classical authors to mean stopping places on a journey. So they conclude that Jesus here is speaking of our pilgrimage to heaven as an ascent undertaken in stages, like the grades through which you have to pass when you learn the piano.

These are all attractive theories, but none of them carry a great deal of conviction with me. By far the most satisfying interpretation of what Jesus means by the phrase is simply that in heaven there is room enough for all. 'Don't worry then, Peter. Life is not like an entrance examination in which you must show yourself superior to everybody else in order to gain one of those places of very limited availability in the higher institution. It is not a competition in which only those who are prepared to be heroes and martyrs have any chance to win. No, for a Christian, heaven is "my Father's house". In other words, it is home. That is how you are to think of it. Heaven is where you belong. Trust God. No, more than that, trust me, for I know what I am talking about in this matter.

'If there was any possibility of any disciple of mine forfeiting his right of abode in the heavenly country, I would have told you about it. Take my word for it, there is a place reserved there for you and for every Christian believer. It is precisely to confirm that reservation that I must leave you now. That is why I do not want you to despair about my going. This parting will not be for ever. Some of you, like Peter, will follow me through the corridor of death later on. You will find me there waiting for you at the other end of that corridor. Some of you perhaps will still be alive when I return to this world on the Last Day to wind up history, and you will meet me that way. It really makes no difference.

'Either way, I am going to make sure of our personal

reunion. If I go and prepare a place for you, I will come back and take you to be with me, so that you also may be where I am. That is a promise. So let there be no fanaticism, Peter. You do not have to die for me; which is just as well, because you will soon discover that right now you could not do it anyway, for all your good intentions. What you have got to do is to trust me. Trust me through the bitterness of these coming days; the bewilderment of disappointment, the tears of failure, the darkness of bereavement. Trust me that I do know what I am talking about and that the path I am treading is not a dead-end, but a through road.'

The question of Thomas—the agnostic

> Thomas said to him, 'Lord, we don't know where you are going, so how can we know the way?' (14:5).

If the reaction of some to bereavement is hysteria, there are others of a more morbid disposition whose characteristic response is to lapse into depression. I suspect that Thomas was one of these. I find something just a trifle amusing about his gloominess. He reminds me distinctly of A.A. Milne's famous donkey, Eeyore. Thomas is so pessimistic about the possibilities of unravelling the mysteries of which Jesus speaks that he shrugs his shoulders in melancholic resignation. His enquiry is not so much a question as an affirmation that all questions are pointless. 'We don't know where you are going, so how can we know the way?'

Far from seeking spiritual illumination, Thomas is in a mood only to exaggerate the hopelessness of the darkness. In short he is an archetypal agnostic, the sort of man who won't take 'Know' for an answer. He gains perhaps some perverse satisfaction from what he takes to be his irremediable ignorance. We cannot know, so what is the point of talking about it?

At least we must compliment Thomas on his honesty.

There are some people who never admit to perplexity
about anything. They always insist they understand. It
would have been very easy for Thomas to have donned such
a mask of superspirituality and made fawning noises of
agreement in this situation. 'Oh, quite so, Jesus. Of course
we know the way you're going. Peter is just a pompous ass,
we are always telling him so.'

The church has more than its share of such spiritual yes-
men, with their plastic piety and boring orthodoxy. They
make life very dull for a pastor. At least Thomas is candid
enough to admit that he has got a problem. There is no
stereotyped testimony of faith to which he feels he has to
conform. If he does not know he will say so, with unrepres-
sed candour and we must conclude from Jesus' uncritical
response to his remarks that he entertained a good deal of
respect for that kind of integrity. Maybe there is, as the
poet says, 'more faith in honest doubt than in half the
creeds'. Certainly Jesus does not rebuke him as an unbeliever because he says he does not know.

But what he does do is to redirect the conversation in a
very thought-provoking manner.

Jesus answered, 'I am the way and the truth and the life. No-
one comes to the Father except through me' (14:6).

Just think about that. Up till now he had spoken of
heaven as the Father's house and himself as the guide to
lead us there. It seems that part of Thomas' confusion was
tied up with the fact that he found it very hard to imagine
the next world as a place like that, or indeed to understand
how anybody could journey there.

Perhaps like many a contemporary rationalist, knowledge for him had to be empirical, scientific, founded on
concrete material realities, not upon abstractions and
metaphors. 'Where is this Father's house, Jesus? The third
street on the right past Mars? And how do you plan to get

there? Rocket ship—or will you beam up, like Captain
Kirk of the starship *Enterprise*? No, all these metaphysics
are too airy-fairy for me. They leave too many unanswered
questions. Let us face it, Jesus, we don't know about this
heaven you talk about. We can't know about such things.
So how can we believe in them, let alone find the way?'

'I am the way!' replies Jesus. 'No-one comes to the
Father but by me.' Do you see what he is doing? He is sub-
stituting persons for places. Instead of speaking of the
Father's house, he speaks to Thomas of going to the Father.
Instead of talking about himself as the guide on that journey, he speaks of himself as the path, the way itself. It is as
if he is saying to Thomas, 'Look, your rationalistic mindset
is taking my physical metaphors too literally. If you find it
hard to think of heaven as a place, think of it instead as a
Person, someone who, far from being unknown to you, is in
fact a familiar face. It is me, Thomas. Think of heaven as
me.

'Your problem, Thomas, is that you do not know me.
You fail to realise what you have got in me. Of course I
have not analysed for you the molecular formula for death
and resurrection; I do not need to. *I* am the way. Of course
I have not derived for you the mathematical equation for
ultimate reality; I have no need to. *I* am the truth. Of course
I have not explained to you the philosophical nature of eternal existence; I do not need to. *I* am the life. Thomas, you
are like a man who complains he cannot get into the car
when all the time the car keys are jangling in his pocket. Do
you not realise that the answer to your agnosticism is staring you in the face? You *do* know the way. If you really
knew me, you would know my Father as well. From now on
you do know him and have seen him. Heaven is not a loca-
tion to which you must journey, Thomas, it is a relationship
with me which you have already begun.'

Let me be frank with any reader who would claim to be
an agnostic, because if you are such a reader then Jesus, in

addressing Thomas' scepticism is saying something of great relevance to you. First of all, Jesus says that you must *take him seriously*. He insists upon it. There are of course many people who make the multiplicity of world religions and philosophies an excuse for their agnostic lack of commitment to anything. 'There are so many different faiths. How can God expect me to know which is the right one, even assuming that he is there at all?' Jesus will not permit that kind of evasiveness. 'I am the way,' he says. 'No man comes to the Father except through me.'

You may speculate all you wish about how God is going to judge the heathen who have never heard of Jesus. The Bible never addresses itself to that question, for a very simple reason. Anybody who carries a Bible in their hand, by definition, does not belong to that company; and since it is not the purpose of the Bible to satisfy mere idle curiosity, it sees no point whatsoever in telling us about how God plans to judge the heathen. If you want to speculate upon that issue then you are free to do so.

What the Bible does make absolutely crystal-clear is that there will be no dissident voices in heaven. There is going to be nobody in heaven saying what a wonderful chap Muhammad is for getting him there. Nobody will be praising the Buddha. The Bible insists that heaven is united by one single chorus of praise, 'Worthy is the Lamb who was slain.' If any heathen is going to be saved, he is going to be saved by Christ. For there is no other way to the Father, except through Jesus. That means, for any agnostic, that whatever religions you may think are worth looking into you cannot afford to ignore Jesus. You have to take him very, very seriously. His exclusive claims demand it.

But Jesus is saying something else very important to an agnostic here, namely that you must not make an *excuse of your ignorance*.

If you really knew me, you would know my Father as well.

From now on you do know him and have seen him (14:7).

Thomas knew more than he knew he knew! And so do you. For though you may call yourself an agnostic, in looking at John's gospel you have come face to face with Jesus.

Of course there are many unanswered questions on your mind, as there were on Thomas's. If you insist that every one of those questions receive a satisfactory answer before you are prepared to call yourself a Christian, you will never find faith. You will die as what you are now, a spiritual 'don't know'. For Jesus is not offering you answers to all your philosophical queries, he is offering himself. According to him, the ultimate truth which you seek is not a system of propositions to be proven by logic and apprehended by intelligence. It is not something for intellectuals only. The ultimate truth behind this universe is personal: it is him.

It is to be apprehended, therefore, in the only way any person can be apprehended, by trust, by love. You may call it a gamble, but then all personal relationships are gambles. Some of you have been married at a church altar saying 'I will'. If that is not a gamble, I do not know what is! Looked at through the tunnel vision of the rationalist mindset, all personal relationships are gambles, and yet without them we beggar ourselves as human beings.

Jesus invites you to take a gamble on him. He does not demand that you switch off your brain and stop worrying about your intellectual problems. He does not insist that you should immediately believe everything that Christians are supposed to believe. He asks only that you believe in *him,* that you identify *him* personally as the source of those answers you seek, irrespective of whether you have clearly formulated those answers yet. He says that without him we have no chance of finding answers at all. 'I am *the* way, *the* truth, *the* life.'

That is why I say that in encountering Jesus, though we may not realise it, the defensibility of agnosticism has

evaporated. From now on, he says, you do know. There
may be some people in this world whose ignorance is excus-
able, but you are no longer among their number. To remain
a 'don't know' after you have come face to face with Jesus
is not an act of religious neutralism. It cannot be. As far as
Jesus is concerned, it is an act of culpable folly.

The question of Philip—the mystic

Philip said, 'Lord, show us the Father and that will be enough
for us' (14:8).

There is a third way in which people sometimes react to
bereavement, other than non-acceptance or depression.
There are some people who turn to the occult. They look
for some kind of direct contact with the world beyond to
confirm its existence. I suspect that Philip rather leans in
that direction. 'Show us the Father,' he says. He wants
some tangible, unmediated experience of God that will
sweep his doubts away. Perhaps he is thinking of a
theophany such as Moses received at the burning bush in
the Old Testament. Or maybe he has been influenced by
the Greek mystery religions and has his mind on some kind
of inner ecstasy, a spiritual trip that will lift him up to new
levels of consciousness.

Either way he seeks for what the medieval mystics called
the *visio dei,* the vision of God. And either way, there is just
a hint of Promethean arrogance in the way that he asks for
it. 'Show us the Father and that will be enough for us.' I am
reminded of the story of Ptolemy of Egypt, who asked Euc-
lid to teach him all he knew about mathematics during his
coffee break. 'Show us the Father and that will be
enough'—enough indeed!

One could not have been surprised if Jesus had replied,
'Don't be such an idiot, Philip. You are asking for the
moon. Every Jew knows that God is invisible.' There is no

such thing as unmediated experience of God, whatever the mystics claim. No man has ever seen God. Yet the interesting thing is that though Jesus does in a sense scold Philip for asking such a stupid question, he does so for totally the opposite reason; not because seeing God was out of the question, but rather because it had already happened and Philip had failed to notice!

> Don't you know me, Philip, even after I have been among you such a long time? Anyone who has seen me has seen the Father. How can you say, 'Show us the Father?' (14:9).

So far we have come across some remarkable claims on the lips of Jesus. But here Jesus is surely making the most astonishing claim of all. 'He who has seen me has seen the Father.'

C.S. Lewis has pungently expressed how unique that claim was:

> If you had gone to Buddha and asked him 'Are you the son of Brahmah?' he would have said, 'My son, you are still in the vale of illusion.' If you had gone to Socrates and asked, 'Are you Zeus?' he would have laughed at you. If you had gone to Mohammed and asked, 'Are you Allah?' he would first have rent his clothes and then cut your head off. ('What are we to make of Jesus Christ?' *in* C.S. Lewis, *God in the Dock: Essays on Theology and Ethics,* Collins.)

But Jesus said, in a voice of calm deliberation, 'He who has seen me, has seen God.' The quest of the mystics for direct experience of God is by his coming rendered redundant. The greatest and most immediate experience of divinity is not to be found by pillars of fire on mountain tops, or spiritual ecstasies while contemplating your navel. It is to be found through him.

It is such a remarkable claim. I know people have problems with what Christians say about the incarnation—God

becoming a human being. But it is no mere piece of dispens-
able mythology, rendered necessary by the limitations of
our human understanding. It is the only way divinity can be
fully expressed, not because of our human limitations but
because of God's nature. The only way a personal God can
reveal himself to you and me is through a Person. There is
no higher way of revealing God than that. Whatever mystical visions and experiences we may be granted, none of
them is higher than meeting Jesus. For they are all sub-per-
sonal experiences. Therefore they must be inadequate. The
only way a personal God can reveal himself totally to us is
through a Person, and Jesus says here that 'that Person is
me'.

In him, Godhead and manhood inextricably intermingle.
In Jesus, God speaks not just through the occasional
inspired oracle but all the time. In him God's works are
constantly to be seen in every action. They are indistin-
guishable from his own.

> Don't you believe that I am in the Father, and that the Father
> is in me? The words I say to you are not just my own. Rather,
> it is the Father, living in me, who is doing his work (14:10).

Inevitably, we demand evidence for such a claim. Jesus
seems to feel that if we were sufficiently in tune with God,
spiritual intuition by itself would confirm his identity to us.
We would hear the ring of truth in his words alone.

> Believe me, when I say that I am in the Father and the Father
> is in me (14:11).

But if you must talk of proof then plenty exists. There are
the signs that he performed, for instance.

> At least believe on the evidence of the miracles (14:11).

If any of us objected that they are all past history now, he would point us further to the continuing signs of his authority within the church.

> I tell you the truth, anyone who has faith in me will do what I have been doing. He will do even greater things than these, because I am going to the Father. And I will do whatever you ask in my name, so the Son may bring glory to the Father (14:12–14).

This verse is the proof text for those who feel that supernatural healings and so on should be a regular feature of Christian experience today. I am personally convinced that miracles do happen, but I am not at all sure that that is what Jesus is saying in this verse, because if you interpret it in that way then it is an embarrassment; it proves far too much. 'Greater things' than Jesus? Does anybody seriously suggest that the church has ever done greater miracles than Jesus did? Greater miracles than raising the dead and stilling the storm and feeding the five thousand? Even the miracles of the early church were far more modest than that.

Certainly no one is performing miracles on that scale today, because if they were you would not be able to get near them for the television cameras. That sort of event does not go unnoticed in our world of mass media. No, we must conclude that when Jesus speaks of 'greater things' here, he is thinking beyond miracles in the narrow sense. He is anticipating what he is going to talk about extensively in the later part of this final discourse, namely the work of the Holy Spirit who could not come until he had gone to the Father.

The Spirit had a greater work than Jesus to do in the sense that his supernatural influence would be spread throughout the world and not merely be localised in one place in Judea. The apostles may not have performed such incredible signs as Jesus did, but on the day of Pentecost, more people were converted in a single hour than were converted throughout the whole course of Jesus' public ministry. I think that if we saw things as Jesus saw them, we would realise that such conversions are far more miraculous than just healing the sick. In fact he more or less said so himself. 'Which is harder,' he asked, 'to say your sins are forgiven you or rise, take up your bed and walk?' (cf. Mk 2:1–12). A modern example is that of the alcoholic who was converted and, having gained victory over his drink problem, began to put his life back together. He got jibed at a lot at work about his faith in Christ. One day his mates were going on about miracles. 'Go on, you don't believe in miracles,' they jeered. 'What about the turning of the water into wine? You've never seen water turned into wine have you?'

'No,' he replied, 'I've never seen water turned into wine. But I have seen beer turned into furniture!'

There are similar contemporary evidences of the divine identity of Jesus all around us. You have only to ask any Christian and they will provide you with personal testimony on the point. And Jesus is performing such life-changing miracles today in the same way he's always done them, in response to personal request.

You may ask me for anything in my name, and I will do it (14:14).

Once again, it is tempting to interpret this as a blank cheque. 'Dear Jesus, please may I have that Rolls Royce?' . . . 'Dear Jesus, please may my premium-bond come up?' But that kind of carte-blanche cannot be Jesus' intention, and he says so when he specifies 'In my name'. The prayers that he promises to answer are those that he would have asked in our place, and which are therefore consistent with his character and purpose.

Actually, it would be no blessing to be able to get anything one wanted anyway. One has only to think of the mischief that results in fairy tales when people have their three wishes granted. We are too fallible to wield omnipotence without God's veto controlling us. Why, if Jesus really promised to give us whatever we asked for unconditionally, the wise among us would never pray again. Rightly understood, 'in my name' is not a limitation but a liberation. It is a glorious incentive for the Christian church to pray without restraint, knowing that we are not working magic spells that could go wrong. We are petitioning a loving and all-wise Lord who never goes wrong.

Ask Christians and they will tell you. Christ is still at work today. Faith for them is not merely a conviction about the past, but an experience of the present. The evidence is there, Philip, if you really must have it. But do not ask for mystical experiences, do not ask that Jesus shows you the Father. If you knew who Jesus was you would be beyond that.

I wonder if someone reading this is wavering. Somebody perhaps who has been thinking about becoming a Christian for quite a long time, for many months, even years and yet never seems to get there. Perhaps you are looking for some kind of wonderful experience that will blow your mind and dispel all your doubts instantaneously. If so, maybe Jesus is saying to you just what he said to Philip. 'Don't you know me? Even after I have been with you for such a long time, do you still not know me? You don't need a mystic experience to become a Christian, for a Christian has something much better than mystical experience. A Christian has me. He who has seen me has seen the Father. Just as Peter had to learn to trust through his failure and Thomas had to learn to trust through his ignorance, so, Philip, you have to learn to trust through your doubts. It is not really so difficult, not if you really know me.'

Yet perhaps your problem is that you do not really know Jesus. Oh, you are familiar with him. But there is a familiarity which is not knowing. If that is your situation, my advice to you is to pick up a Bible and start reading the gospels.

You could start by reading the rest of the gospel of John. That is where you will meet Jesus. Their purpose is to introduce us to him. Saturate yourself in his words, in his deeds. And while you read about him, pray. Pray in his name that if he is real, he will show you the divinity in himself. He says, 'He who has seen me, has seen the Father.' There is no way of seeing God better than that.

Surely God is not playing hide-and-seek with you. If you really do want to find him, you will. It is just a matter of looking in the right place, that is all. Jesus says, 'I am the way.'

8

The Bequest

''Tis better to have loved and lost, than never to have lost at all.' No, that was not quite the way that Tennyson wrote those famous lines! It is an intentional mis-quote by the satirist Samuel Butler, designed to make the worldly-wise amongst us smile.

But do you think it could ever be true? Do you think that losing someone we loved could ever seriously be regarded as preferable to not losing them? It is hard to believe so. There are few sadnesses more profound than a lovers' farewell, and the more permanent the farewell the more intense the sadness. Parting is only a sweet sorrow when, like Romeo and Juliet, you anticipate meeting again the following day. When the parting admits of no such early reunion, then it's hard to discover any sweetness in it at all.

We may smile at Samuel Butler's cynical wit. But the truth is that any love that considers itself fortunate to have lost rather than to have kept its beloved cannot be real love at all. As far as real love is concerned, anything is preferable to separation. That is why the vow has to be 'Till death us do part'. That is why bereavement, of all the experiences of life, is so disturbing to our emotions, plunging even the sanest of us into depths of depression. For those who know what love is all about, there is surely nothing at all positive about having loved and lost.

Yet Jesus in John 16 insists that there is; at least, as far as he is concerned.

I tell you the truth: It is for your good that I am going away (16:7).

We must remember that Jesus speaks these words on the very threshold of his own arrest and execution. He is walking with his disciples towards the Garden of Gethsemane, a stroll all too familiar to them, but which he was taking on this occasion for the very last time. And he knows it. Again and again he talks about his departure. 'I'm going away. I'll only be with you a little longer. You will not see me again.' The more he has spoken like this, the more morbid and melancholy his disciples have become. When their conversation began, back in the Upper Room, they were full of questions, even objections.

But as the evening has worn on, this note of imminent departure has continually threatened the conversation, and their despondency has grown deeper and deeper. They have had less and less to say. The discourse has taken on more and more the nature of a monologue, so much so that even Jesus himself confesses that he is finding their gloomy silence depressing.

Now I am going to him who sent me, yet none of you asks me 'Where are you going?' Because I have said these things, you are filled with grief (16:5–6).

Now his opportunity to speak to them is almost at an end. There is much more he would like to say but their faces betray their inability to cope with it at the moment. So Jesus must bring his long farewell to a conclusion. Before he does so, however, he tries to get them to look on the positive side of what is about to happen. 'I want you to realise,' he explains, 'that losing me is not the disaster that you think it is. On the contrary, rightly understood it constitutes a blessing. If you only understood a little more, you would realise that it is better to have loved me and lost me than never to have lost me at all.'

Of course, self-pity often blinds us to the hidden purposes of God in our sad and tragic experiences. But of no-one was that more true than these disciples. Their melancholy was particularly inappropriate.

> Unless I go away, the Counsellor will not come to you; but if I go, I will send him to you (16:7).

Jesus is sure that someone will come to compensate them for his loss. 'He is my bequest to you.' Who is he? A little earlier in this farewell discourse Jesus had already identified him.

Who is this 'Counsellor'?

> I will ask the Father and he will give you another Counsellor to be with you for ever—the Spirit of truth (14:16–17).

> All this I have spoken while still with you. But the Counsellor, the Holy Spirit, whom the Father will send in my name, will teach you all things (14:25–26).

Now of course there was nothing novel about the Spirit of God as far as these disciples were concerned. They were perfectly familiar with the idea from their reading of the Old Testament. Even the title 'Holy Spirit' was not new to them. However, with only the Old Testament to go on, one could perhaps have forgiven these disciples for thinking of the Holy Spirit as a some*thing* rather than a some*one*. For when you read the Old Testament that is quite often how it seems to be. The Spirit is a kind of creative energy flowing out from God, communicating his intelligence and his power to the universe and sometimes to human beings too. But he is not very clearly indicated as a person.

Indeed, up until this point in Jesus' ministry nothing he had taught the disciples would have changed that impression very dramatically. He had spoken of the Spirit as being the agent whereby devils were cast out. He had spoken of the Spirit of God as anointing him for his special mission. Perhaps the disciples already knew that Jesus' human nature had been conceived by the Spirit of God in the womb of Mary. But there would be nothing in all of those things to disturb their essentially Old Testament understanding of the Spirit. In fact the Spirit had been a very minor feature in Jesus' ministry up till now, hardly ever mentioned at all.

But as we stand at this point in the Gospel narrative we are on a momentous threshold. A great revolution is going to take place in this respect. On the evening of his departure, Jesus introduces the Holy Spirit to his disciples in a radically new and much more central way. No longer was he a something. He was a Someone, a distinct Person in his own right, with a most distinct role in their lives. Nothing makes that clearer than the name Jesus coins for him, 'the Counsellor'.

The Greek word behind that title is *parakletos,* which literally means someone who is called in to assist. In the ancient world, the word was most commonly used in a legal context. If you were brought to trial your *parakletos* might be your lawyer. Or he might be a witness in your defence, or possibly just a friend who had come along to give you moral support in court. Whatever specific role such a 'counsellor' fulfilled, however, one thing is self-evident. A *parakletos* was always a person, never a thing. John, in fact, goes out of his way to emphasise that fact by his conspicuous use of masculine pronouns in this text. Although it is difficult for us to see it in translation, there is a very good example in verse 26. John uses a very emphatic (and grammatically unnecessary) masculine pronoun in that verse: '*He* will teach you all things.' It is as if, by his defiance of

normal grammatical convention, John wants to say to us:
'Look, "Spirit" may be neuter in Greek vocabulary, but he
is personal in Christian experience—A "he" not an "it".'

It is vital we realise that. For today in spite of the huge
amount of attention that is given to the Holy Spirit in some
respects, I am not at all sure that our interest always treats
the personality of the Holy Spirit as seriously as it ought to
do.

Quite often today the central idea in people's minds
when they talk about the Holy Spirit is 'power'. That is of
course a word that you certainly come across in the New
Testament. But it has dangers. For 'power' suggests a kind
of divine electricity, something impersonal which, perhaps,
we can tap at will and make use of. The book of Acts tells
the story of someone called Simon Magus who seems to
have made precisely that mistake. He thought of the Holy
Spirit in just that way and was rebuked for it. For the fact is
that we cannot use the Holy Spirit. If we understood the
personal nature of the Spirit more fully we would realise
why it is impossible. My old colleague, Gottfried Osei-
Mensah, once used a splendid illustration in this regard. He
said, 'Suppose someone sent you an explosive bomb
through the mail. You would have to decide how you were
going to dispose of it. Suppose on the other hand, an Afri-
can dictator were to come to visit you at your house, it's
much more likely he would decide how to dispose of you!'

So God has not promised us impersonal parcels of
power. He has promised us a powerful Person, the Spirit.
He is not at our disposal. We are at his. We do not use him.
He uses us. If we receive him, it is not because we have mas-
tered some religious technique for tapping his power, but
because Christ has interceded on our behalf with the
Father.

> I will ask the Father and he will give you another Counsellor
> (14:16).

Who is he then? He is nothing less than a divine Person, and we must constantly guard our hearts against the sub-Christian tendency to de-personalise him.

What does he do?

> I will ask the Father and he will give you another Counsellor to be with you for ever . . . . I will not leave you as orphans (14:16, 18).

The Spirit then compensates us for the physical absence of Jesus. One of the platitudes which C.S. Lewis tells us he found very difficult to take from his Christian friends when his wife died was what he calls the 'pitiable cant' of those who said: 'She will live for ever in my memory.'

> *Live?* That is exactly what she won't do. You might as well think like the old Egyptians that you can keep the dead by embalming them. Will nothing persuade us that they are gone? What's left? A corpse, a memory . . . . all mockeries . . . . more ways of spelling the word *dead*. It was H. I loved. As if I wanted to fall in love with my memory of her, an image in my own mind! It would be a sort of incest. (*A Grief Observed*, Collins.)

This is pungent writing. But of course he is right. Sentimental memories make it harder, not easier, to come to terms with loss. They encourage us to live in the past, or worse still to fantasise about it, when what we really need is help to face up to the reality of our new loneliness. It is the presence of the loved one we crave, not just their memory. Jesus understands that as he speaks here. Of course memories are important. In point of fact he has just instituted a feast of bread and wine which his disciples would regularly observe 'in remembrance of me'. Without such memories, the rootedness of our faith in history would be in jeopardy. Christianity would be reduced to just another kind of religious mysticism. But while memory is important, memories alone are not enough. In fact, on their own they can be just a frustration rather than a help. It is the personal presence of Christ in our lives that we need to dispel our sadness. That is precisely what he promises us here.

Do you notice that word 'another'? *Another* Counsellor. What does he mean by that? One recalls Alice at the Mad Hatter's Tea Party, who made the point that you cannot be offered more tea unless you have drunk some already. In the same way, Jesus can hardly speak of another Counsellor, unless there has been a predecessor. Who is this predecessor? Read the passage and it becomes clear: it is Jesus himself. Up till now he had been the disciples' *parakletos*—their Friend, their Supporter, their Advocate, their Helper. But now he was going to the Father, and Someone else would continue to exercise that personal role towards them.

At least, I say 'Someone else', but in fact that may be too strong a phrase. For do you notice in the passage how subtly Jesus passes from the third person into the first person when he talks about this Counsellor?

> The Spirit of truth. The world cannot accept him, because it neither sees him nor knows him. But you know him, for he lives with you and will be in you. I will not leave you as orphans: I will come to you (14:17–18).

Has Jesus made a subtle shift between verses 17 and 18? Is he talking about something new when he says '*I* will come to you'—is he talking about the second coming, perhaps? Or is he saying that when the Holy Spirit comes to the disciples, in some sense he comes too?

There can be little doubt, I think, taking this final conversation with his disciples as a whole, that it is the latter which is chiefly in his mind. Indeed you could make a good case for saying that the Holy Spirit in this passage is thought of simply as Jesus in another form.

In his incarnate nature, Jesus could only be *with* them. But as the Spirit—the Counsellor—he will be *in* them (14:17). As the man from Nazareth he could be their companion for only *a little while*. But as the Spirit, he would be at their side *for ever* (14:16). In his physical body, he was visible to *the world* at large. But as the Spirit, he would be perceptible only to *his disciples* (14:19).

There are, it is true, great dangers in speaking of the Spirit as Jesus in another form. Specifically, there is a danger called modalism, a heresy which confuses the Father, the Son and the Holy Spirit and which speaks of God as if he were an actor, who exchanges roles or wears different masks at different times. That clearly cannot be right, because the Father and the Son and the Holy Spirit co-exist in this passage and have relationships with one another. The Spirit is distinct from Jesus. He is *another* Counsellor. And the Spirit is distinct from the Father, for Jesus must pray the Father to send him. Yet such is the mystery of the Trinity that it seems that in giving us the Spirit, God is giving us Jesus as well. That is, of course, why the Church Father Tertullian could speak of the Spirit as the Vicar (or deputy) of Christ; and that is why, when you read the rest of the New Testament, you find that the early Christians do not make any clear distinction between the Spirit of God and the Spirit of Jesus.

It is a tremendous truth we find here, then. Jesus is not going away at all. In a very real sense he is still going to be around. He will remain our companion. He offers us here something much better than memories. He even offers something better than sacraments. He offers us the indwelling presence of his own Spirit.

'The Spirit will be a positive improvement on my physical presence among you. One of the major reasons I am leaving is precisely so that he may come to you.'

An obvious question we want to ask Jesus is why we cannot have our cake and eat it: 'Why can't we have the Holy

Spirit and you simultaneously?' Jesus does not answer that question here. John commented on it back in chapter 7, throwing a little light. 'The Spirit up to that time had not been given,' he wrote, 'because Jesus had not been glorified.' All we can say with certainty is that what Jesus was about to achieve by his dying on the cross, rising from the dead and ascending to glory was a vital preliminary to the Spirit's release. In the diary of God's eternal plan, Easter had to be over before the Day of Pentecost could arrive.

Some people have suggested that Jesus' death on the cross was no more than a mere martyrdom. Clearly in his own mind it was far more than that. It was an event of cosmic significance which marked the threshold of a whole new era in God's relationship with men. The age of the Spirit was about to dawn and only the presence of the risen and glorified Jesus in heaven could secure its commencement. 'If I go, I will send him to you.'

The change would have momentous consequences both for the world and for the church. Consequences so immensely valuable, they would render his departure, not a tragedy at all, but an advantage.

The Holy Spirit's work in the world

> When he comes, he will convict the world of guilt in regard to sin and righteousness and judgment: in regard to sin, because men do not believe in me; in regard to righteousness, because I am going to the Father, where you can see me no longer; and in regard to judgment, because the prince of this world now stands condemned (16:8–11).

If we are honest, we have to admit that there are elements in this paragraph which are cryptic, even a little mysterious. They have led to a fair amount of debate in the commentaries but I do not want to get engaged in too much of that, because the general thrust of the verses is clear.

Jesus is saying that it is the distinctive work of the Holy Spirit to awaken a sense of moral shame and spiritual concern in human hearts. Why is it that a person who has lived a whole lifetime of careless indifference to God can suddenly be arrested by a sense of sin, and discover an urgent need to find personal salvation?

Jesus says it is the work of the Holy Spirit. It is he who 'convicts the world of sin, righteousness and judgement'. That word 'convict' is a technical word in Greek legal language, meaning the cross-examination of a hostile witness. It is a very appropriate choice of vocabulary, because you may remember that the Counsellor (or *parakletos*) was originally a friend in a law court who gave you personal support when you were on trial. What Jesus is saying in these verses, then, is that the Holy Spirit not only fulfils that role, speaking words of encouragement and consolation to the hearts of Christian believers when they are on trial by the world, but he also goes on the offensive. He also challenges the consciences of unbelievers. He is not just a defence lawyer. He is the public prosecutor who convicts the world of its guilt.

But somebody may ask, is that really *new*? Haven't people always been convicted of their sins, before Jesus as much as after? Surely the Holy Spirit has always been doing that, rebuking men's evil and holding that evil in check? Of course he has. But if you look carefully at Jesus' words, you will see that, with this new release of the Spirit that will result from his departure, a radical change in the nature of that convicting work of the Spirit takes place.

First of all, Jesus says there will be *a new focus for the definition of sin*. He will convict men of sin, not merely because they break the Ten Commandments, but 'because they do not believe in me'. From now on it is the rejection of Jesus which ultimately damns the world. Contempt for God's law can be forgiven. Contempt for his Son cannot. It is the Holy Spirit's work to expose to men and women the

moral and spiritual rebellion that hides behind the mask of
their unbelief.

Secondly, there will be *a new certainty about the vindica-
tion of righteousness*. He will convict the world in regard to
righteousness, but not merely because God's standards are
eternal. Now he has something else to wield, 'because I am
going to the Father'. It is the exaltation of Jesus which from
now on guarantees the triumph of goodness in the world.
There is no doubt any longer about the kind of life-style
that is going to last, and which will be honoured in eternity.
It is the life-style of Jesus, the risen Lord. It is the Holy
Spirit's work to convince men and women that there is
something absolute and inescapable about the moral claim
which Jesus makes upon us.

Thirdly, according to Jesus, there will be *a new urgency
about the imminence of the end of the world*. He will convict
the world of judgement, but not merely because sometime
in the indefinite future God is going to call the universe to
account. The Old Testament Prophets could have said that.
But now there is something new: 'the prince of this world
stands condemned'. That is a perfect tense not a future. We
are no longer talking about some far off Day of the Lord,
but about *now*. The devil's attempt to usurp the throne of
the universe is already confounded. With the exaltation of
Christ, the kingdom of God has arrived. The messianic
reign the Prophets spoke about is here. Judgement is no
longer a distant threat, but an imminent crisis. Each of us
must take sides now, for this victorious Jesus or for his
defeated enemy. It's the Holy Spirit's distinctive work to
inject that imperative call for decision into our consciousness.

Do you see what I mean when I say that in every way the
convicting work of the Holy Spirit is enhanced, improved
and rendered more compelling by the departure of Jesus?
Before Jesus went away, vast multitudes of the human race
successfully ignored God's claim upon their lives. Yet on

the day of Pentecost alone, three thousand men were cut to the heart by the Apostle's words. Why? Because the Holy Spirit had come, convicting the world. And so it has gone on; the influence of Jesus is one million times greater today, two thousand years after his death, than it was during his own lifetime. For the Holy Spirit, the Counsellor, has convicted the world of its guilt.

So there is immense encouragement in these words if we grasp them and really think about them. Firstly, there is encouragement to those Christians who are particularly concerned about *social justice and moral standards in the world,* for there is nothing in these verses which specifically says that the Holy Spirit performs this work of conviction only in those who are about to be converted.

Many people have limited it to that application, but the text does not actually warrant such restriction. The world he convicts is *still* in its state of unbelief and hostility. The implication is that, just as there was a general influence for good upon the consciences of men and women in Israel as the result of the propagation of the Ten Commandments through Moses, so we may anticipate that the world at large will be permeated by a new moral dynamic as a result of the ministry of the Holy Spirit. We may expect to see people persuaded of the rightness of Christian values and the dignity of Jesus Christ, even though they do not always personally embrace him as their Saviour.

To put it another way, we do not have to give up on secular society and just concentrate on the church. The Holy Spirit is active *in the world,* convicting it of sin and righteousness and judgement. The prince of the world is judged. Christ is exalted as Lord over the world. So the world must be the orbit of Christian action, not just the church.

Secondly, there is immense encouragement in these verses to those who are involved in *the development of Christian apologetics* (the study of how to convince people). As

far as Christianity is concerned, people need convincing of
two things. They need convincing negatively, of the futility
of non-Christian ideas; and positively, of the correctness of
Christian ideas.

There is a superb example of apologetics in Paul's famous sermon to the Athenians. But I am afraid apologetics is
a pursuit which quite a few people nevertheless disparage.
Right-wing fundamentalists tend to do so because they
claim it is too philosophical. 'You cannot convince anybody
by debate or by reason,' they argue. And it is disliked by the
more liberal wing of the church because they feel it is con-
tentious. 'We ought to be concentrating on what great religions have in common, not making a fuss about our differ-
ences.'

Suffice to say, that the Holy Spirit is on the side of
apologetics. The word 'convict', which Jesus uses, clearly
has the meaning of persuading people by argument that
their ideas are wrong and that they need to be changed. If
the Holy Spirit is engaged in such apologetic activity on
behalf of Jesus in the world, surely we should be too.
Indeed it is only because he is so active that we dare to try.

Thirdly, I find great encouragement in these verses personally. It can be quite a disheartening thing to be a
preacher. 'How can I persuade these people that they need
to change?' you ask yourself. One feels so helpless and
inadequate. After all, the Marxist terrorist can pick up a
machine gun and hijack an aeroplane to get his message
spread around the world on prime-time television, but all the
preacher can do is preach. It seems rather ineffectual in the
1990s. Often a voice whispers in one's ear, 'You're just wast-
ing your breath, you know.' But I know that is not true. I
know that the conscience of everyone who hears preaching is
on the preacher's side. An invisible advocate is at work con-
firming the authority of the message of Jesus to their hearts.
Indeed there is not one of you who will finish reading this
book as an unbeliever without consciously suppressing or

subconsciously repressing the challenge of his inner voice. Not one of you. Your conscience is on my side too!

I hope that is an encouragement to some of you. Maybe you have sensed that inner prompting that I am describing. You have felt an intuitive conviction about your own moral state and about the significance of Jesus, and the urgent need for decision in his favour. But perhaps you have been inclined to be suspicious of those feelings. You are tempted to put it all down to your over-religious upbringing, or even to the emotional impact of the writer's eloquence! You have told yourself not to take all this stuff too seriously. 'It's all imagination,' you say to yourself.

Well, I am the last person to encourage you to be gullible or naive in this matter, but I do want you to know that there is another possible explanation for the inward pressure which you feel towards Christian commitment. It could be nothing to do with your religious upbringing at all. After all, that has not bothered you much before has it? It could be nothing to do with the writer's eloquence. It could be that the Holy Spirit himself is challenging you, calling you to repentance and faith. If it is, then you should be grateful, because Jesus is telling us here that even if you had Jesus himself, in his physical presence before your eyes, he would not communicate so great a persuasion of truth as the invisible presence of his Spirit is doing right now in your heart.

The Holy Spirit's work in the church

> I have much more to say to you, more than you can now bear. But when he, the Spirit of truth, comes, he will guide you into all truth. He will not speak on his own; he will speak only what he hears, and he will tell you what is yet to come. He will bring glory to me by taking from what is mine and making it known to you. All that belongs to the Father is mine. That is why I said the Spirit will take from what is mine and make it known to you (16:12–15).

I suspect that Jesus never spoke any more important or

potentially dangerous words. They are important, of course, because they explain why Jesus never wrote anything down. Most of the Prophets considered their message important enough to get it down on paper for the benefit of subsequent generations. Some of them were even told by God to do it. But Jesus never seems to have bothered, in spite of the fact that he clearly believed his authority was supreme. He never picked up a pen, because he anticipated the ministry of the Holy Spirit within his followers. It would be his Spirit's distinctive task to perpetuate the special revelation he had brought after his departure.

It is precisely here that the danger lies. For many would seize on these verses as proof of a continuing gift of inspiration in the church, in consequence of which we may rightly expect new revelations of the Holy Spirit even today.

As popular as such interpretations of Jesus' words are—in certain quarters anyway—they are not really substantiated by the rest of the New Testament. I want to suggest to you that we must observe a vital distinction between the application of these words to Christian believers generally, and their application to those to whom Jesus spoke them in the first place.

It is important to remember that when Jesus uses the second person plural 'you' throughout this discourse, he is not speaking directly to you and me but to the eleven disciples, who were accompanying him on his journey towards Gethsemane. Of course, it is perfectly true that the vast majority of what he says is also relevant to us because those eleven disciples were the embryo of the church. What was true for them as first generation Christians is, 90% of the time, true also for us their twentieth-century successors. But we must not jump to the conclusion that *everything* Jesus says to them he also intends to say to us. There are points in this conversation which are not transferable in that way.

Let me illustrate that by reference to chapter 14.

> The Counsellor, the Holy Spirit, whom the Father will send in
> my name, will teach you all things and will remind you of
> everything I have said to you (14:26).

Now the Holy Spirit cannot remind *us* of what Jesus said
in the same way that he could remind the Apostles, for the
simple reason we never heard Jesus speak in the flesh in the
way they did. That verse clearly meant something for them
which it cannot mean for us.

The same applies to 15:26–27:

> When the Counsellor comes, whom I will send to you from the
> Father, the Spirit of truth who goes out from the Father, he will
> testify about me; but you also must testify, for you have been
> with me from the beginning.

Once again, the Holy Spirit cannot accompany our testimony to Christ in quite the same way he could accompany
that of the Apostles, for the simple reason that we were not
eyewitnesses of Christ as they were. We were not with him
'from the beginning'; that was their special privilege. Once
more, that verse clearly meant something for them which it
cannot mean for us.

It is important to realise then that throughout this sermon Jesus' primary reference is the eleven, and only by
extension is what he is saying applicable to us.

That is vital when you read this promise of the revelation
of new truth after Jesus' death; truth which he had not been
able personally to teach in his lifetime because of the disciples' limited spiritual capacity at that time.

This new truth will have two characteristics, he tells us.
Firstly, it will be truth regarding *the future*: 'He will tell you
what is yet to come.' Almost certainly, that is not to be
understood in the very narrow sense of predictive
prophecy, for the New Testament sees the coming of Jesus
as the birth of the Messianic Age. 'Things to come' have

arrived in Jesus. That is probably what he is referring to here. He is saying that the Spirit would guide them into the full significance of the new age which was dawning with his cross and resurrection and ascension.

Secondly it will be truth regarding *Jesus himself*: 'He will bring glory to me by taking what is mine and making it known to you.' In other words the whole theological understanding of the church would be deepened as a result of the Holy Spirit's clarification of the person and the work of Jesus. Every aspect of our knowledge of God would be developed and reshaped by the christological perspective. Jesus promises a major reconstruction of our religious understanding after he leaves the world.

But it is simply not true that such new truth is still being discovered today by the church. The promise of inspiration, which Jesus is making here, is exclusively directed to the Apostles, not to us. In fact if you read Jesus' words carefully that is implicit in them: 'He will guide you into *all* the truth,' he says, not *some* of it, but *all* of it. It is not a case of first generation Christians being given a bit of the truth, and then subsequent generations of the church filling in more and more of the picture. Jesus' promise is that the Holy Spirit would give a *total* revelation to the Apostles themselves. And that is certainly the way in which they themselves understood it.

You do not find the Apostles at the end of the first century telling the church to look for more inspired apostles and prophets who will continue to expound new truth. Instead you find them warning in the severest tones about the danger of false prophets, and urging the church to transmit faithfully that body of gospel teaching which they, the Apostles, had once and for all delivered to the saints. In the Book of Revelation you even find the church likened to the City of Jerusalem with its walls built on the twelve Apostles. The apostolic company is the foundation of the church. These first-generation Christians have a quite unique place in the development of Christian doctrine. Jesus here is not promising us all access to new revelation through the Spirit, but teaching us rather about the special character of apostolic authority. Those whom he is here appointing to that special office would be channels of new revelation through the Spirit.

They had been with him from the beginning. They would be reminded of what he had said, so that they would not only write reliable accounts of his life and ministry, but would be inspired by the Spirit to understand far more about Jesus' significance than he had ever been able to share personally with them during the days of his flesh. Jesus is, in other words, anticipating in this verse the birth of the New Testament.

Are we then to say that these verses have no relevance to us? Are we to read them solely with the Apostles in mind? Should we think of the Spirit as guiding *them* into all the truth, revealing Jesus to *them*, bringing glory to Christ through what he showed *them*? Certainly, that is the primary reference, but it would not be true to say that there is not some application by extension. For though there was a unique ministry of the Holy Spirit to the Apostles, it does not mean, of course, that there is no ministry of the Holy Spirit to our understanding of God's truth as well.

It is quite clear from the rest of the New Testament that he does indeed *illumine* the minds of Christians generally as they read the Apostles' writings. Paul even goes so far as to say that without the help of the Holy Spirit we just cannot get to grips with New Testament revelation. According to him, people without the Spirit are unable to accept the things that come from the Spirit of God. They are foolishness to them. They cannot understand them. So, in that more limited sense, Jesus' words are applicable to all Christian believers, including us.

But in the days in which we live it cannot be stressed enough that this *illumination* by the Spirit is very different from *inspiration*. Inspiration is the gift of understanding new truth. Illumination is the gift of understanding old truth. That is why the Apostles' sermons go into the Bible and mine had better come out of it. Here, then, is the second great advantage the Holy Spirit brings. He works not only in the world to convict it of sin. He works also in the church to bring us instruction. And in both cases, he works far beyond anything we could have had before Jesus' departure.

It is crucially important that we grasp this last point, because it explodes all kinds of fallacies. It exposes the futility of the 'quest for the historical Jesus'. There are some liberal scholars, although not as many as earlier in the century, who think they are doing us a service by paring away the gospel narratives in order to get rid of all the bits which the disciples added, so that we can just get down to the 'original Jesus'. Of course this is pure nonsense. There is no Jesus except the Jesus to whom the Spirit and the Apostles testify. The hard truth is that the Apostles understood Jesus a thousand times better after he had gone than they did while he was still here. This was not because they had the leisure then to invent a new theology, but because they then had the Holy Spirit to impart new truth about him.

You find a similar kind of fallacy among some evangelical Christians. Have you ever come across a red-letter New Testament? You do not see them so much these days, but they used to be popular. Everything Jesus said in direct speech was printed in red, as if to suggest that those words that came direct from his lips, had more authority and importance than other words in the New Testament text. You still find some Christians confused on that point. But again it is nonsense. The words which the Holy Spirit speaks through the Apostles are every bit as authoritative as those of Jesus. Jesus himself said so. Indeed, such is the manner in which Jesus has chosen to inspire the gospels, that there is often no certain way of distinguishing the original words of Jesus from the later words of the Holy Spirit through the evangelist. Nor is there any point in trying to distinguish them.

But perhaps the commonest fallacy that Jesus dismisses here is what I would call the fallacy of Christian nostalgia. I am sure that you have come across those Christians who are for ever going on about their visit to Palestine. 'It brought it all to life,' they say. 'It was so wonderful to just sit there on the Mount of Olives, and in the Garden Tomb!' I am sure that kind of visit can indeed be an encounter with the Lord. But we do not need the nostalgia of such pilgrimages. If the truth were known, even if we could have sat with the disciples on the hillside and heard the words of the Sermon on the Mount from the mouth of Jesus, we would not be more blessed than we are when we sit with the inspired record of that Sermon before our eyes and the Holy Spirit in our hearts to interpret it to us.

There is no greater blessing than the blessing of the Holy Spirit. Even if we could travel in Doctor Who's time machine back to first-century Palestine, and see the Baby in the manger or the Man on the cross, we would not be spiritually better off than we are now when we hold a New Testament in our hands. We must understand that. 'It is to your advantage I go away,' says Jesus, 'for the Holy Spirit will come.'

So now we see Jesus' reason for telling us that as far as he is concerned, it is better to have loved and to have lost him.

If I am honest, I have to say that it is possible to make too much of the Holy Spirit. There are churches where one hears an awful lot about the Holy Spirit and very little about the Bible. I hope that what I have written here has exposed the fallacy in that. Similarly, there are some churches where you hear an awful lot about the Holy Spirit and very little about Jesus. But these verses make very clear the mistake in such an emphasis. According to Jesus, the Holy

Spirit is the most modest and self-effacing of all the Persons of the Trinity. 'He will bring glory to me,' says Jesus. The Holy Spirit has no interest in talking about himself. He is only interested in talking about Christ. So find a church that makes much of Jesus and you may hope to find a church full of the Holy Spirit. Find a church that makes much of the Spirit to the neglect of Jesus and you are very likely to have found a church that is full of little more than hot air.

But I must also make clear that it is far more lethal an error to make too little of the Spirit than it is to make too much. Show me a church centred around the sacraments, with no real awareness of the Holy Spirit, and I will show you a dead church. Show me a church obsessed with theology and with no real awareness of the Spirit, and I will show you an equally dead church. It is the Holy Spirit who brings the church to life. For it is he who turns Jesus from being a mere hero of the past, commemorated in our books and in our rituals, into our living contemporary.

If it is a choice between standing amongst those crowds who saw him in first-century Palestine, and standing in the congregation of a twentieth-century church, the wise among us will choose the latter. We have no need for nostalgia.

He is the one Person in the world whom it is better to have loved and lost. For if the truth were known, through the ministry of the Holy Spirit, we have not lost him at all.

Epilogue

Every author has a purpose in mind when he writes. It may be to teach, or to entertain, or even the mercenary desire to make money. The apostle John does not leave us in ignorance of his purpose.

> Jesus did many other miraculous signs in the presence of his disciples, which are not recorded in this book. But these are written that you may believe that Jesus is the Christ, the Son of God, and that by believing you may have life in his name (20:30–31).

I have tried to make John's purpose my own too. Inevitably I have been selective in the parts of his gospel which I have examined, just as he was selective in the parts of Jesus' life he chose to record. There is much more that each of us could have said. But our common goal has been to bring within a manageable compass material on the person and teaching of Jesus that will be of help to those who are seriously considering placing their faith in him.

Maybe you are just such a person? As you have read and become familiar with Jesus, the Holy Spirit has been convincing your heart and mind, just as he promised he would. What should your response be? Where do you go next?

May I make a few suggestions?

1. You have an important decision to make; are you ready to become a follower of Jesus or not? It is vital that you

do not equivocate about that matter too long. Of course you will want to think about it carefully. But remember what Jesus said in John 8 about the nature of truth:

> If you hold to my teaching, you are really my disciples. Then you will know the truth, and the truth will set you free (8:31–32).

Christianity can't be proved first and then practised afterwards. Assurance of the truth of Jesus' claims only arrives fully after we are committed to him. Go back to chapter 5 of this book and read about that again if necessary.

2. You have some important things to say; are you ready to confess to Jesus the mistakes of the past and accept the changes he will want to introduce in your behaviour and ambitions? It is not a cheap thing to become a Christian. Remember how Jesus forced the Samaritan woman to face up to the moral failure of her life. He was equally frank with his disciples about the practical obligations that anyone who followed him must take on board:

> If anyone loves me, he will obey my teaching (14:23).

Are there things you can identify in your life that you know Jesus would wish to see changed? Then one of the first steps of faith you will make is to ask him for the strength you will need to make those changes.

3. You have an important company to join; are you ready to involve yourself publicly with the Christian church and be recognised by your family and friends as a believer? It can never remain a secret for long, once someone has found faith in Jesus. We may come, like Nicodemus, in the privacy of the darkness, but he will

not allow us to remain there. As he told his disciples during that final conversation he had with them:

> When the Counsellor comes, whom I will send to you from the Father, the Spirit of truth, he will testify about me; but you also must testify . . . (15:26–27).

It is part of the Holy Spirit's work to enable us to confess our faith bravely to others, even though this may sometimes be a most costly step. For some of us it may mean baptism or confirmation. For all of us it certainly means opening our mouths and telling somebody about the experience we have had, the decision we have made, the faith we now share.

4. You have an important relationship to enjoy; are you ready daily to spend time with God and develop an intimate friendship with him through prayer and the study of his Word? John knew when he wrote his gospel that not everybody who read it would become a believer. Jesus himself was rejected by many of those with whom he came most immediately in contact. There is a mystery here, the mystery of that new birth which he told Nicodemus about. But one thing John is certain about is that some will believe. And that those who do, enter upon a most special privilege:

> He was in the world, and though the world was made through him, the world did not recognise him. He came to that which was his own, but his own did not receive him. Yet to all who received him, to those who believed in his name, he gave the right to become children of God (1:10–12).

If you have made that important decision and put your faith in Jesus, then God has adopted you into his own family. You belong to him now in a way you have never belonged to him before. A marvellous adventure lies in front of you as you begin to explore that relationship. This is the very stuff of which eternal life is made—for this is a relationship you will go on enjoying and deepening for ever. Start right now—with this simple prayer.

> Father God, thank you for working the miracle of the new birth in me. Thank you for the gift of faith that you have awoken in my heart. Thank you for making Jesus real to me through your written Word. Thank you that, though I cannot see him, by his Spirit I can still experience his presence within my life.
>
> Today I want to commit myself to him and become his true disciple. I know there are things in my life that do not please you. Help me, as I determine to try to put them right. Give me the courage I need too, so that I may tell others of what you have done for me. I want to be part of your church and to demonstrate by my obedience to all Jesus' teaching that my commitment is true. As I do that, Father, will you keep close to me and show me day by day more of your love.

Not there yet? But you would like to be perhaps? Don't give up the search! Doubt is not the opposite of faith—but despair is. Before you put this book down read one more section of John's gospel. It may encourage you to persevere when the faith which others have discovered seems to elude you. It need not elude you for ever.

> On the evening of that first day of the week, when the disciples were together, with the doors locked for fear of the Jews, Jesus came and stood among them and said 'Peace be with you!' After he said this, he showed them his hands and side. The disciples were overjoyed when they saw the Lord.
>
> Again Jesus said, 'Peace be with you! As the Father has sent me, I am sending you.' And with that he breathed on them and said, 'Receive the Holy Spirit. If you forgive anyone his sins, they are forgiven; if you do not forgive them, they are not forgiven.'
>
> Now Thomas (called Didymus), one of the Twelve, was not

with the disciples when Jesus came. So the other disciples told him, 'We have seen the Lord!'

But he said to them, 'Unless I see the nail marks in his hands and put my finger where the nails were, and put my hand into his side, I will not believe it.'

A week later his disciples were in the house again, and Thomas was with them. Though the doors were locked, Jesus came and stood among them and said, 'Peace be with you!' Then he said to Thomas, 'Put your finger here; see my hands. Reach out your hand and put it into my side. Stop doubting and believe.'

Thomas said to him, 'My Lord and my God!'

Then Jesus told him, 'Because you have seen me, you have believed; blessed are those who have not seen and yet have believed.'

I Want To Be A Christian

by J.I. Packer

What does it mean to be a Christian? Do you understand the faith to which you have been called?

Dr Packer shows how both *belief* and *behaviour* are changed by true biblical faith. Looking carefully at the Apostles' Creed, the meaning of baptism, the Lord's Prayer and the Ten Commandments, he provides a masterly guide to Christian faith and practice.

Additional Bible passages and questions are included to help with both individual and group study.

J.I. PACKER is Professor of Systematic and Historical Theology at Regent College, Vancouver, Canada, and the author of many books on the Christian faith, including *Knowing God* and, more recently, *Among God's Giants*.

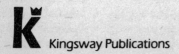
Kingsway Publications